"Let them give glory to the Lord and proclaim
His praise in the islands."
—Isaiah 42:12

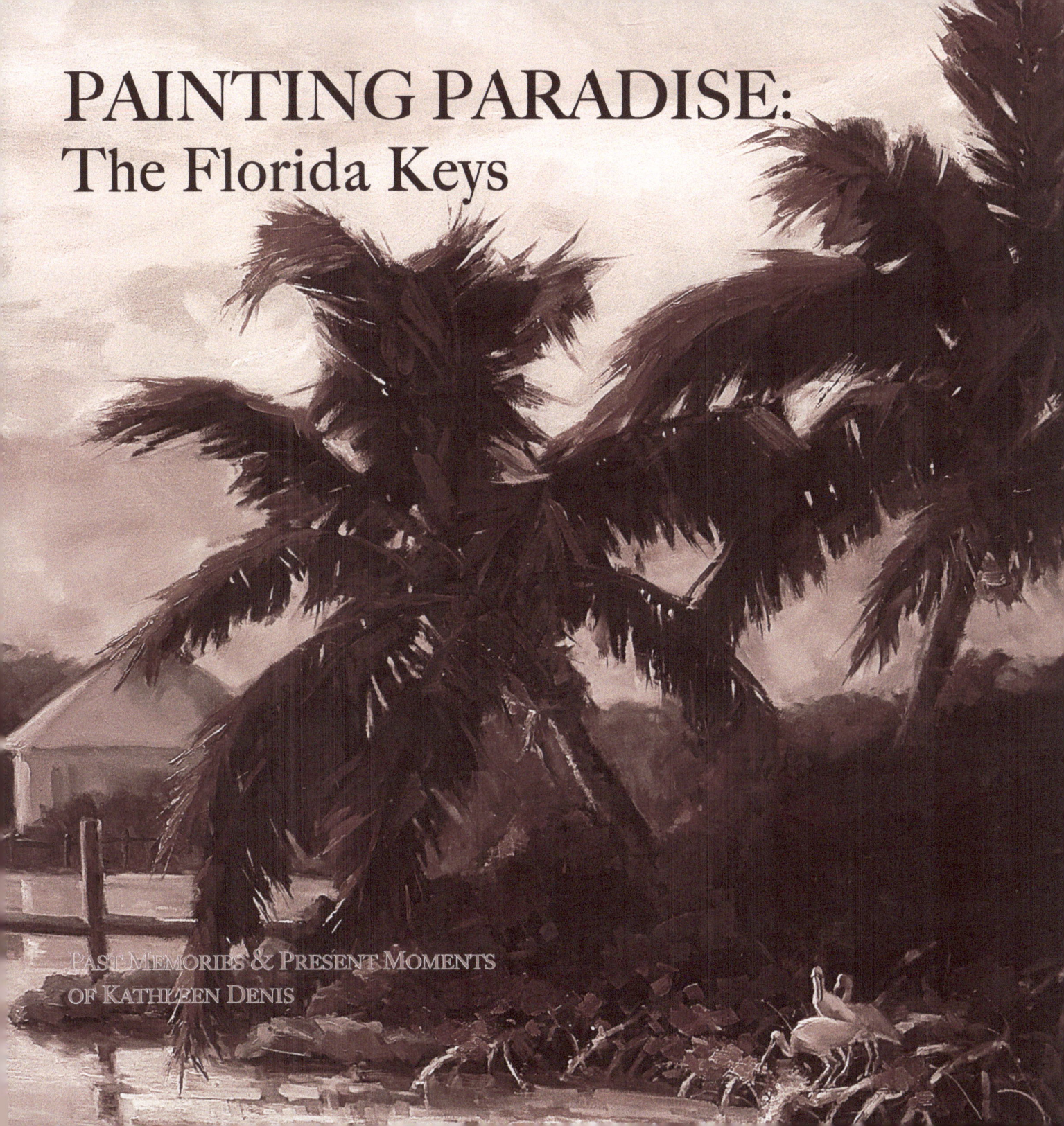

PAINTING PARADISE:
The Florida Keys

PAST MEMORIES & PRESENT MOMENTS
OF KATHLEEN DENIS

PAINTING PARADISE:
The Florida Keys

Past Memories & Present Moments

Book Editing & Design by: Maritza Cosano
Maritza@littleredrockingchair.org

ISBN-13: 978-0-692-60982-8
Painting Paradise: The Florida Keys
Info@KathleenDenis.com
KathleenDenis.com/blog
KathleenDenis.com

Printed in U.S.A.

Dedication

To Jesus Christ, my Lord and Savior, who lets me hold the brush;
without Him none of this would be possible.

To my husband Jeff, for his continuous unconditional love and support, who
patiently finds paint everywhere and "burnt offerings" for dinner,
yet still helps me live my dream and believes in me when I don't.

To my friends and family for encouraging me and understanding
when I can't hang out because I'm painting.

To my mom and dad, for their never ending sacrifices,
specifically by providing me with art classes, beginning at the age of four and beyond.
Dad has passed and mom can no longer comprehend,
but I know in my heart they would be proud of my accomplishments.

"Humanly speaking, it is impossible. But with God everything is possible."— Matthew 19:26

Kathleen Denis

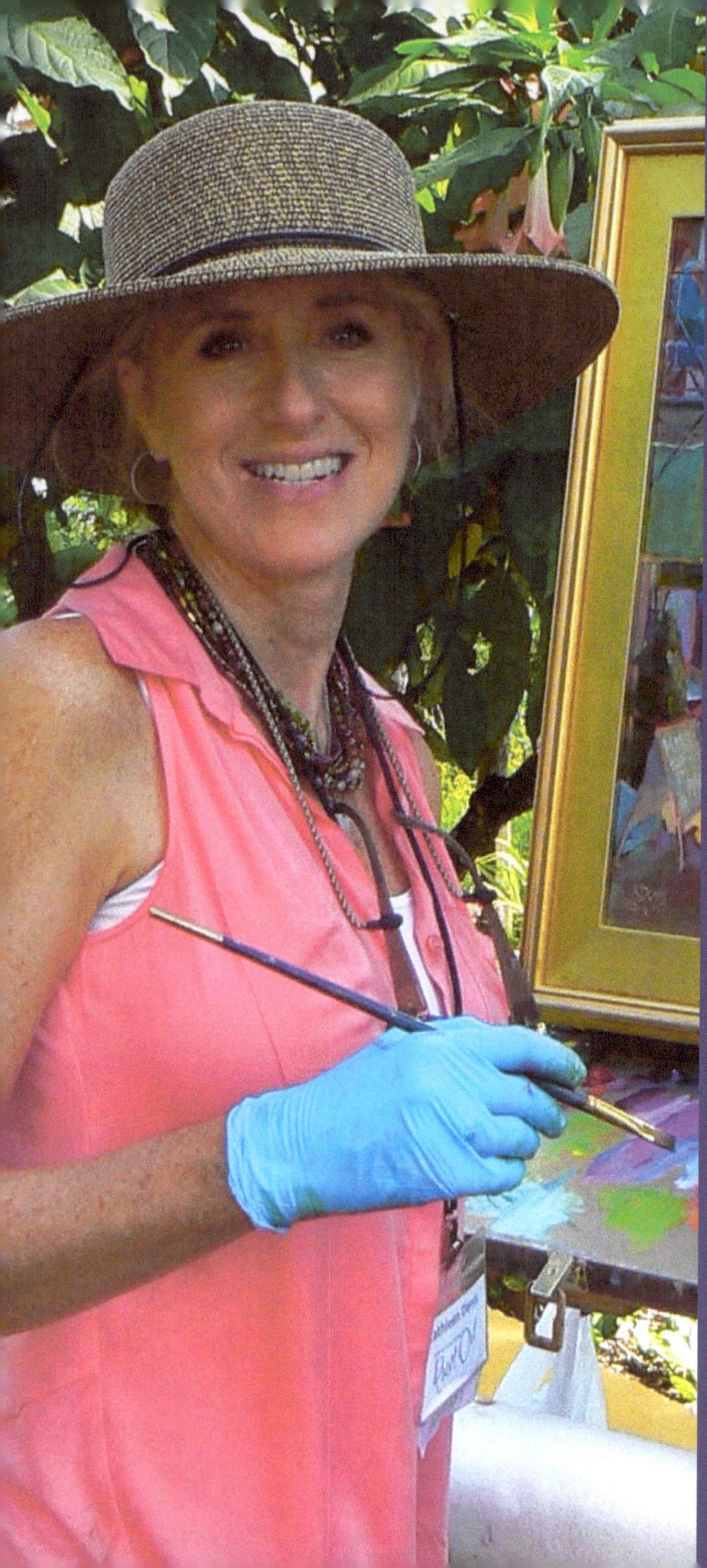

INTRODUCTION

For me, life without painting is like a fish without water. I love to paint and cannot imagine my life without it. My passion began with my first art lesson at four years old, but interestingly enough, most of my childhood was not spent in front of a canvas, but in a studio, training to be a ballerina.

My dream to dance professionally ended upon entering the 11th grade, when I stopped taking dance classes. While in college, I returned to my desire to be an artist and having graduated from University of Miami with a BFA in graphic design, I began using my creativity within the commercial design industry.

My longing to paint intensified while visiting various art festivals in my community and so began my journey into the fine art world as I eventually left the graphic design field to pursue painting. This new endeavor consisted of exhibiting originals and prints in outdoor art festivals, galleries and tradeshows, eventually establishing Kathleen Denis Designs, managed by my devoted husband Jeff. My art was soon discovered by a company that applies images to home décor and gift products, such as flags, floor mats and tote-bags. With that newfound recognition, a kitchen hard-goods company learned of my art and applied it to dishes and other kitchen accessories. Shortly thereafter, a major wallpaper company introduced a full book of my images to the industry, which began an unexpected and exciting career as a "Licensed Artist." Becoming one of the leading nationwide artists in this field, my images were now selling on numerous home décor and gift products by manufacturing companies worldwide.

After many years as a successful licensed artist, a longing grew to use my art to minister hope to others. As a result, I painted a series entitled A Scream For Silence and founded a non-profit organization called, Door of Hope Outreach. These God-inspired paintings (found on my website) present Scripture based elements as visible reminders of His personal love, instruction and power. At that time, I put my brushes down for some years while using these paintings to teach Bible studies in jails, youth detention centers and churches to women in need of hope and restoration.

Then the unexpected desire to paint returned. However, I decided this time to create what inspired me instead of what companies required for the commercial industry. Embracing the oil medium instead of watercolors, and incorporating a more painterly and impressionistic style, a renewed love and passion for painting led me into an inspiring, new chapter as an artist.

During a vacation in Apalachicola, Florida, I experienced my first "plein air event" (the term referring to painting "in the open air") at the Forgotten Coast Paint Out. I found it to be incredibly fascinating and the feeling of excitement drove me to return home and begin my new adventure into plein air painting, with the goal of entering Plein Air Paint Outs. French Impressionist painters such as Claude Monet, who advocated "en plein air" painting, most assuredly experienced the same peaceful sound of birds chirping and the feel of a welcomed breeze, while observing and capturing the colors and nuances distinct to each scene.

Plein air painting includes various interesting and incredible challenges, which serve to captivate me. Whether it's moving vehicles, canvases blowing over, annoying bugs, sunburned skin, heat exhaustion, shivering hands in the cold, or people asking questions such as "are you painting?"—these all occur while having about a three-hour span to capture the essence of the scene before the sunlight changes, clouds invade, or the rains come. When asked how long it takes to paint a scene, I might say three hours, but in actuality it's taken a lifetime.

I presently paint "en plein air" as well as in my studio, appreciating and enjoying both. My work is exhibited through galleries, plein air paint outs and my website, while licensed home decor products and posters may be found by searching the internet under Kathleen Denis and the desired product. Having studied under noted instructors, I fervently impart my artistic knowledge to students through weekly classes and workshops.

I once heard something very profound: "To be an artist, you must paint." Ah, so simple yet so true. It takes an amazing amount of time and practice to become an accomplished artist, therefore, I make every effort to paint daily. I treasure the gift given me and when I paint, I feel the presence of God in my life. I often like to think He just lets me hold the brush.

"Art washes away from the soul
the dust of everyday life."
–Pablo Picasso

LOVE LETTER
16X12,
OIL ON PANEL

LOCATION:
BEACH STREET,
OLD TAVERNIER

Old Tavernier has
some charming
historic homes
that I always enjoy
painting. This one,
located at the end
of Beach Street on
the ocean, I'm told
was the first Post
Office in Tavernier,
hence the name of
my painting, "Love
Letter."

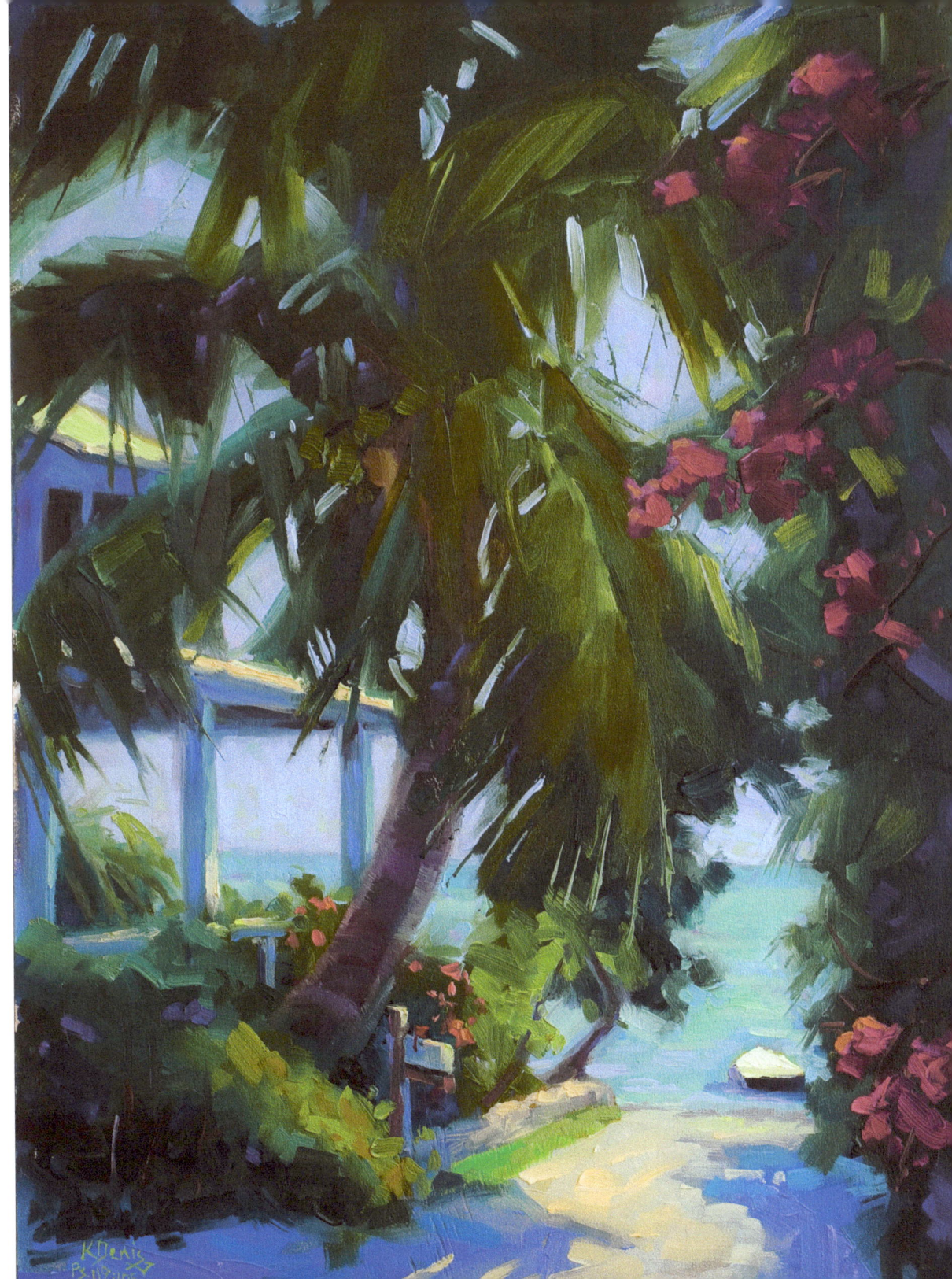

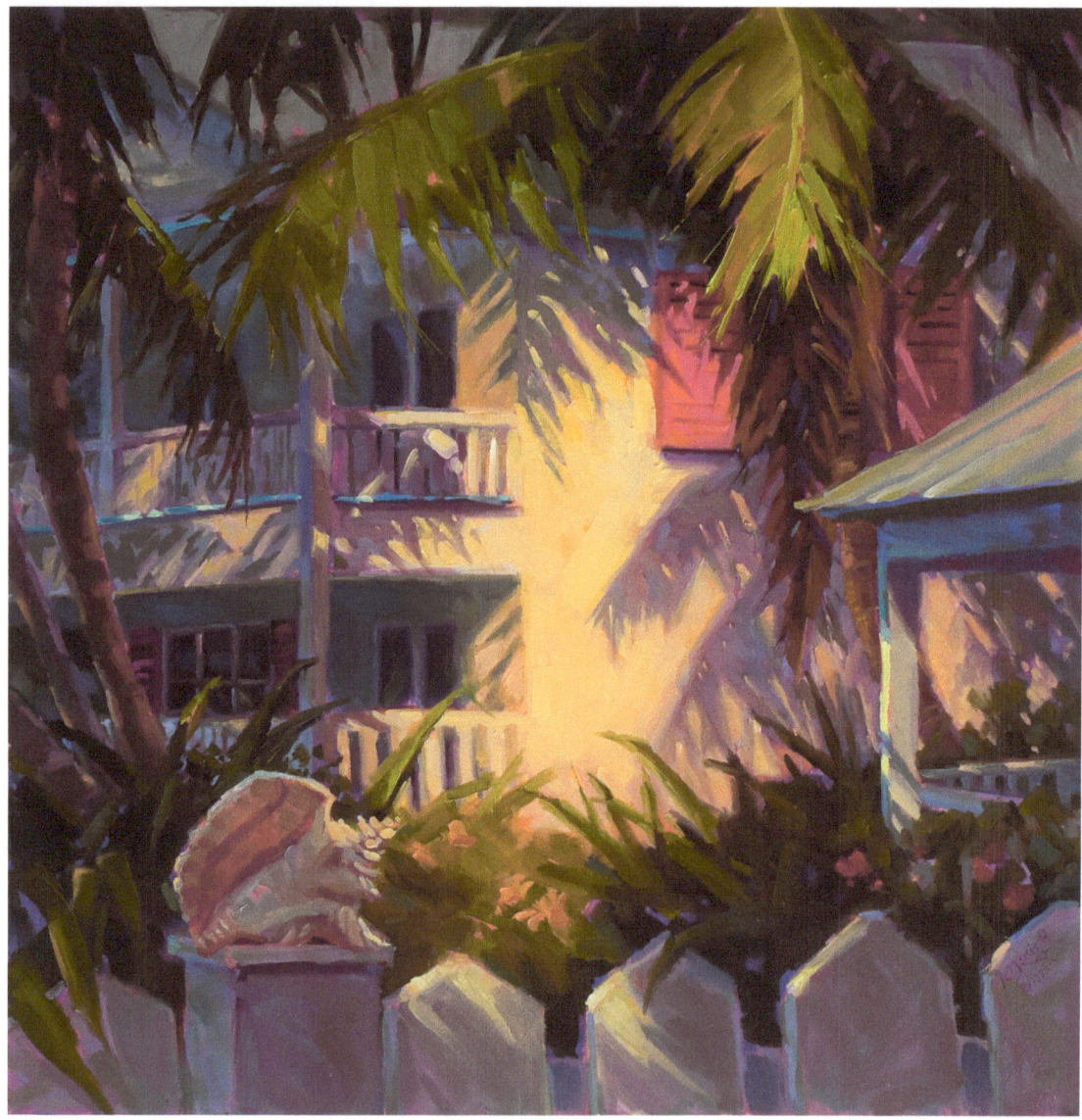

HIDDEN TREASURE
30X30,
OIL ON PANEL

LOCATION:
THE MOORINGS
VILLAGE RESORT
– 123 BEACH RD,
ISLAMORADA,
MILE MARKER 81,
OCEANSIDE

Breathtaking. Just a simple word to describe this tropical *hidden treasure*. This unique luxurious resort is located on a former 18-acre coconut plantation and adorned with old-conch style cottages amidst a canopy of palm trees. Having had the privilege of painting there for many years, I am always inspired by the native island ambiance.

[OPPOSITE PAGE] **PRETTY IN PINK** 30X30, OIL ON PANEL

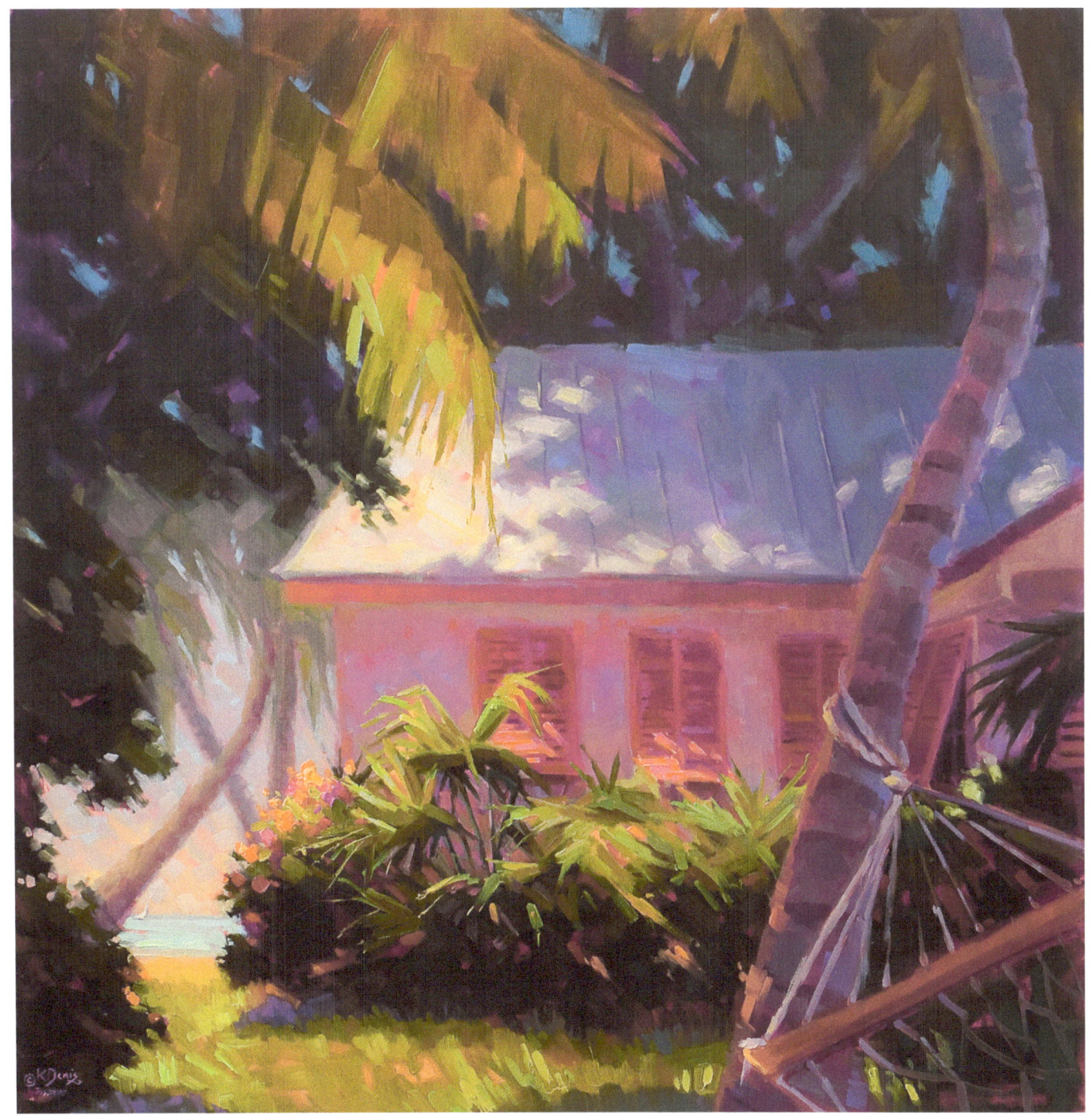

Kathleen Denis

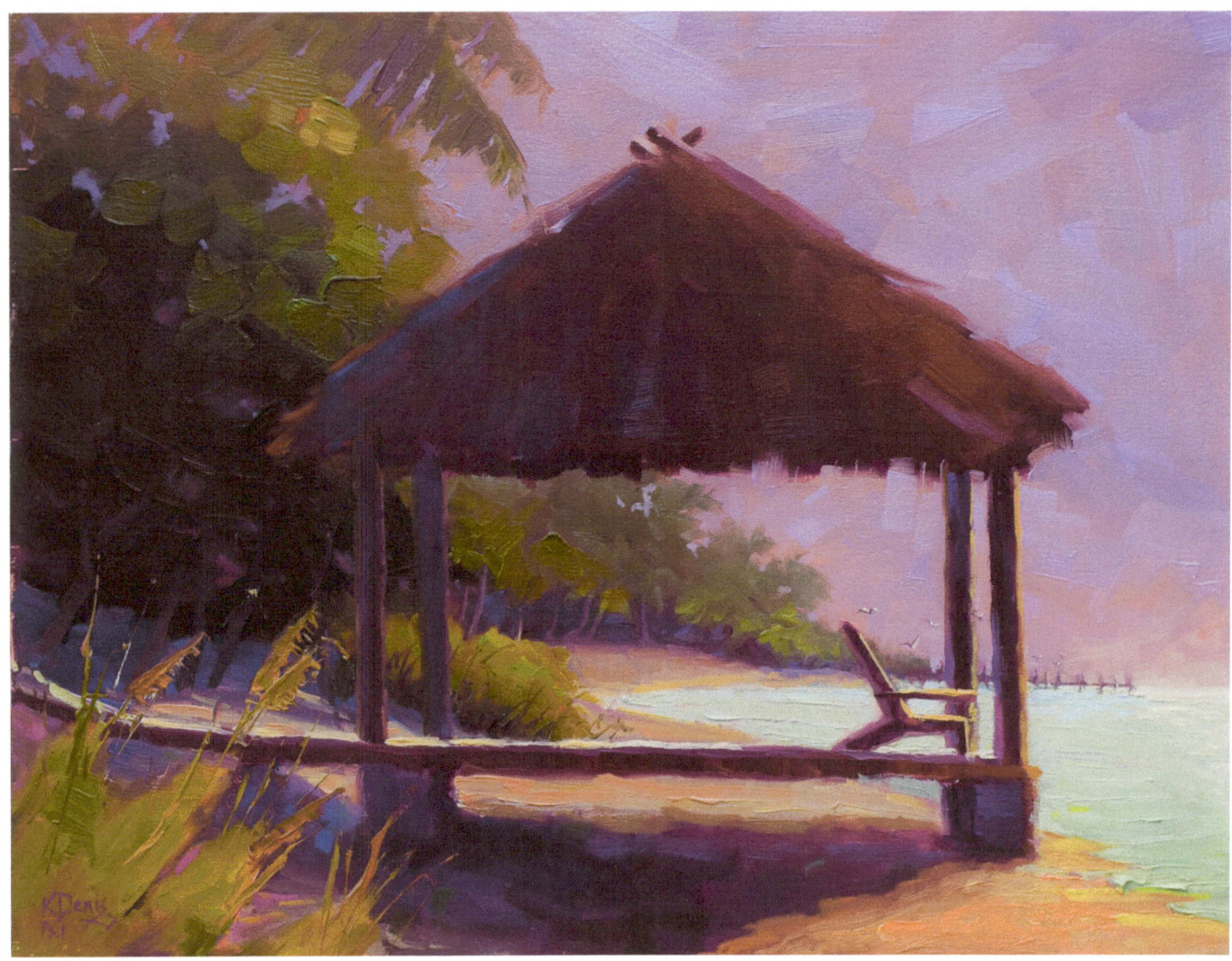

ON THE EDGE 12X16, OIL ON PANEL

LOCATION: PRIVATE BEACH, ISLAMORADA

Some of the most interesting scenes are found down unassuming streets, which was the case for this scene I found in Islamorada. As this chair sits *on the edge* of the dock, it reminds me of how plein air painting is like living on the edge —thrilling and adrenaline driven.

ISLAND SHADOWS
OIL ON PANEL, 48X36

LOCATION:
ANGLER'S REEF
COMMUNITY, ISLAMORADA

Interesting shadows created from the tropical flora are, to me, as stunning as the plants and trees themselves.

My desire in each scene is to capture the intense effect created by light and shadows, producing a mood that intrigues and invites the viewer inside.

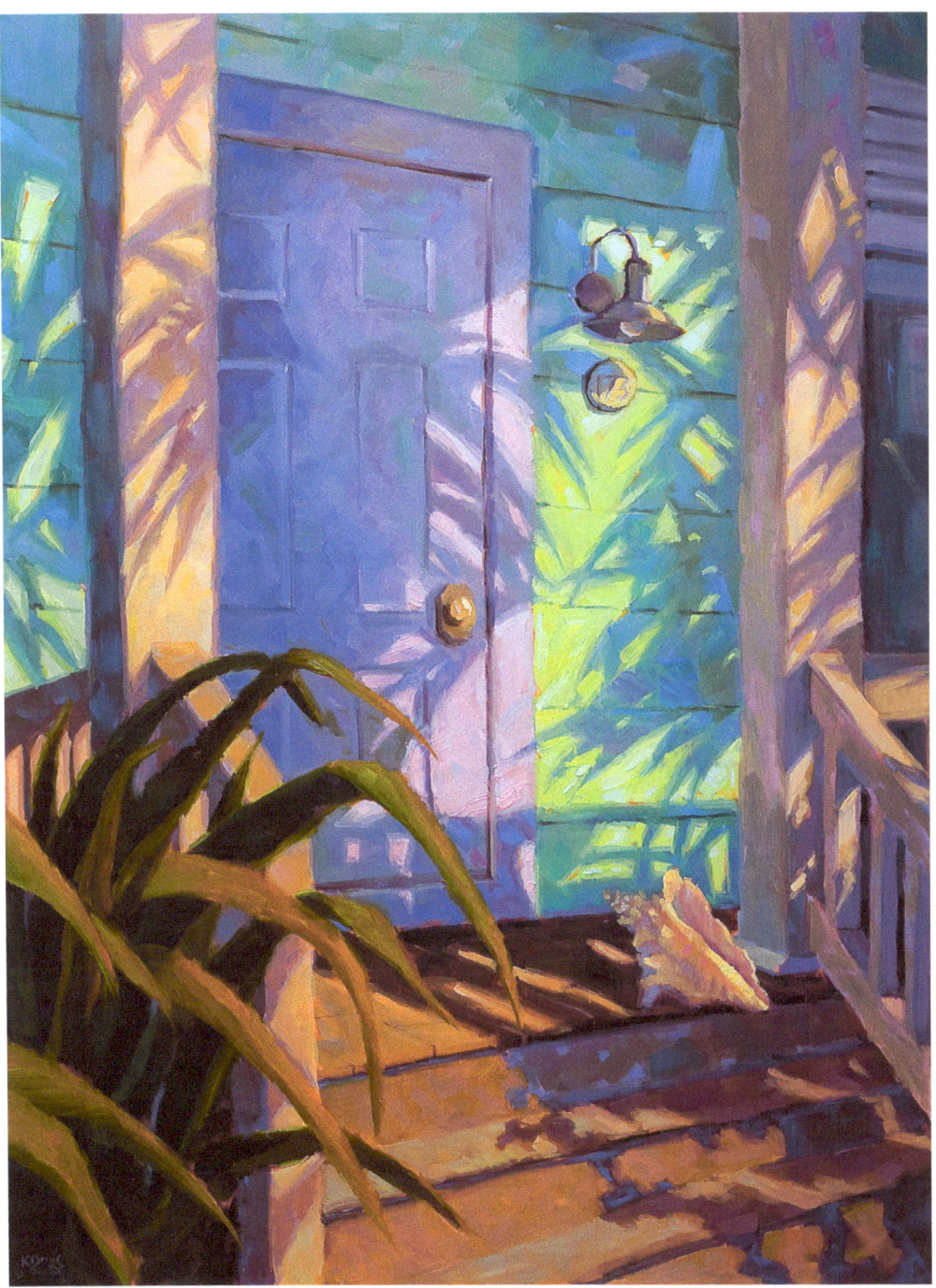

Kathleen Denis

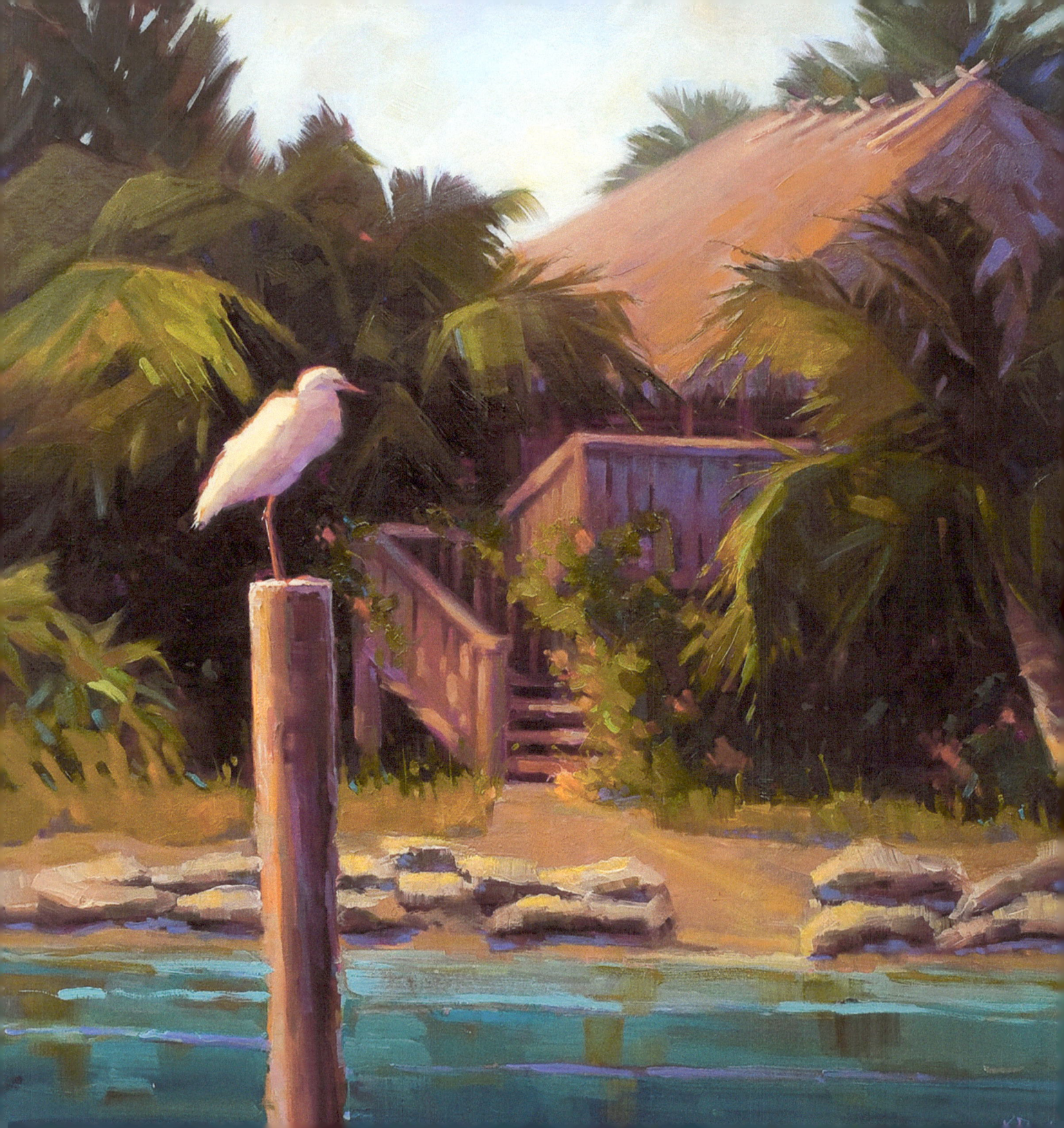

[OPPOSITE PAGE]

BIRD'S EYE VIEW
24X24, OIL ON PANEL

LOCATION: LITTLE PALM
ISLAND
28500 Overseas Hwy,
Little Torch Key

This unique resort, including
colonial-chic bungalows, is located
on a 5 1/2 acre exclusive island,
with 360 degrees of captivating
waterfront views. With access
only by sea-plane or boat, and a
policy of no phones or televisions,
it allows for an ambiance of a
genuine island lifestyle.

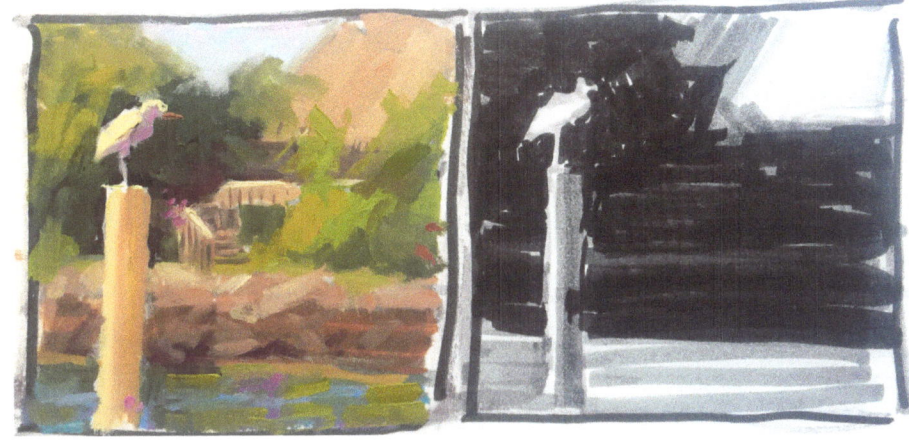

THUMBNAIL SKETCH AND COLOR SKETCH
Before committing the paint to the canvas I worked out these small thumbnail value
sketches and color sketches. These are my "blueprints" for the painting in which I
continue to refer back to as I proceed.

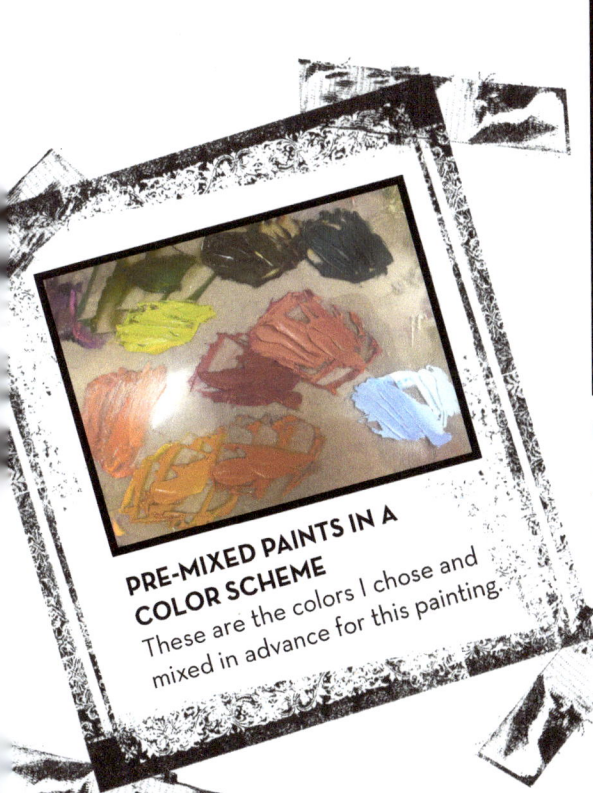

**PRE-MIXED PAINTS IN A
COLOR SCHEME**
These are the colors I chose and
mixed in advance for this painting.

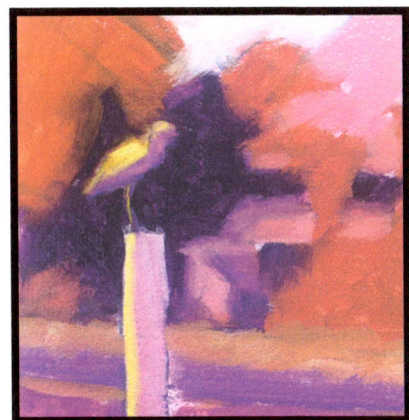

BLOCK IN COLORS
Before putting the "local" colors on
the canvas I first painted these "block
in" colors.

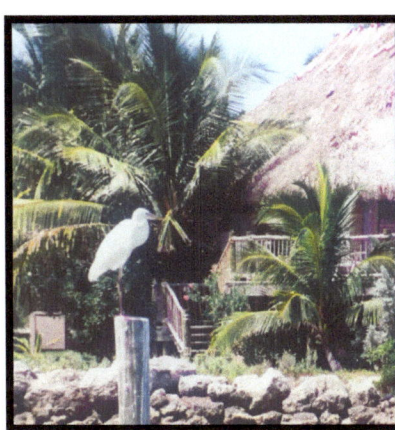

LITTLE PALM ISLAND RESORT
I shot this photo several years ago at
Little Palm Island.

Kathleen Denis

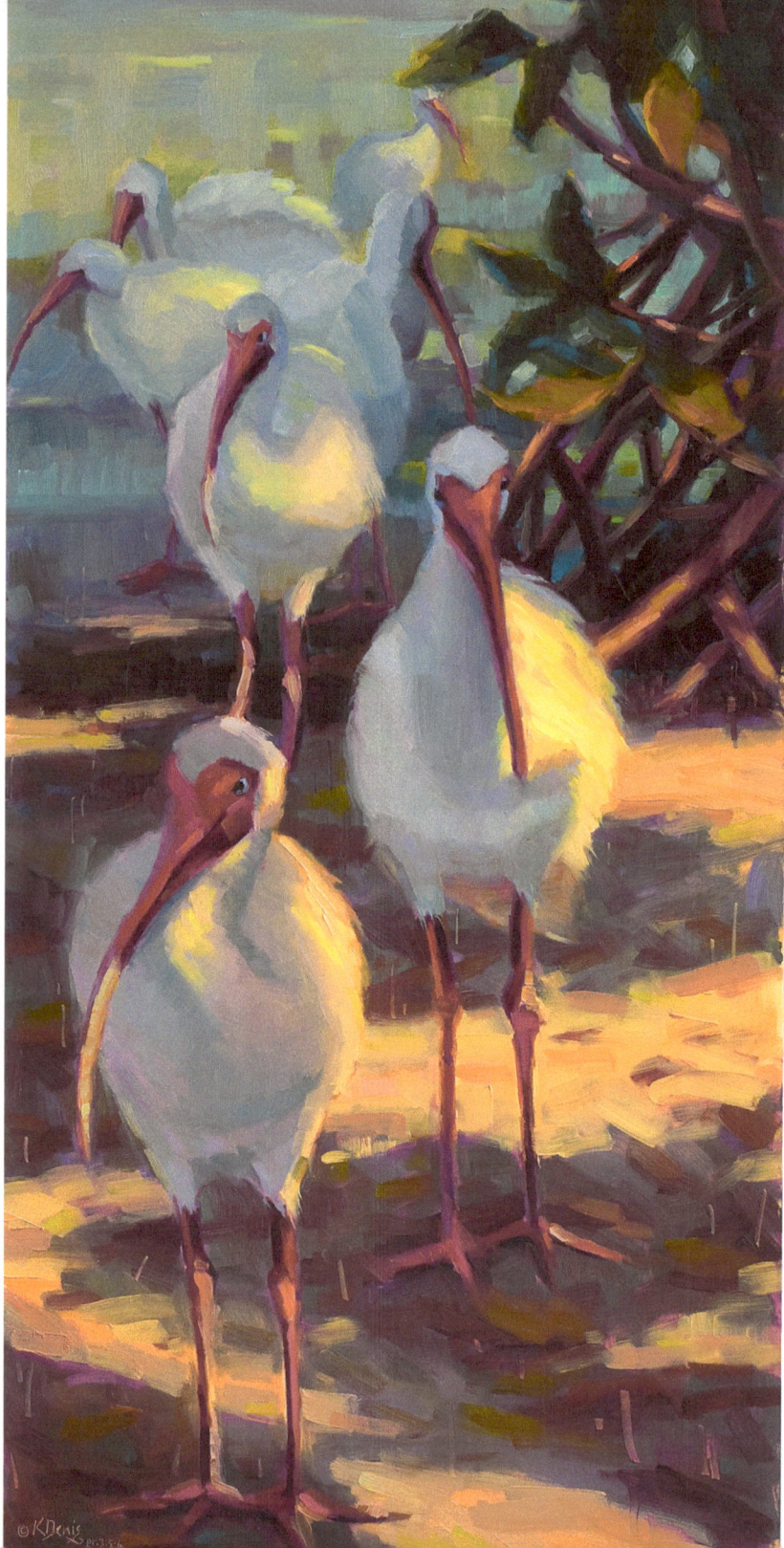

FOLLOW THE LEADER
36X18, OIL ON PANEL

LOCATION:
FLORIDA KEYS WILD BIRD CENTER,
93600 OVERSEAS HIGHWAY, TAVERNIER

If you love birds, you will enjoy seeing the love given to the injured birds at the Florida Keys Wild Bird Center, where I took this photo. These visitors, who aren't injured, apparently also enjoy hanging out there.

WATERFRONT VIEW 24X24, OIL ON PANEL

LOCATION: PLANTATION KEY,
MILE MARKER 89

"Someday I'm going to paint this scene," I said with every visit to my dear friends and neighbors, Keith and Linda. Their backyard sits directly on the bay, daily displaying never-ending spectacular views. Well, here you have it! My heart aches because this precious couple no longer lives here, but fills with joy as I still reflect on their love for God and others.

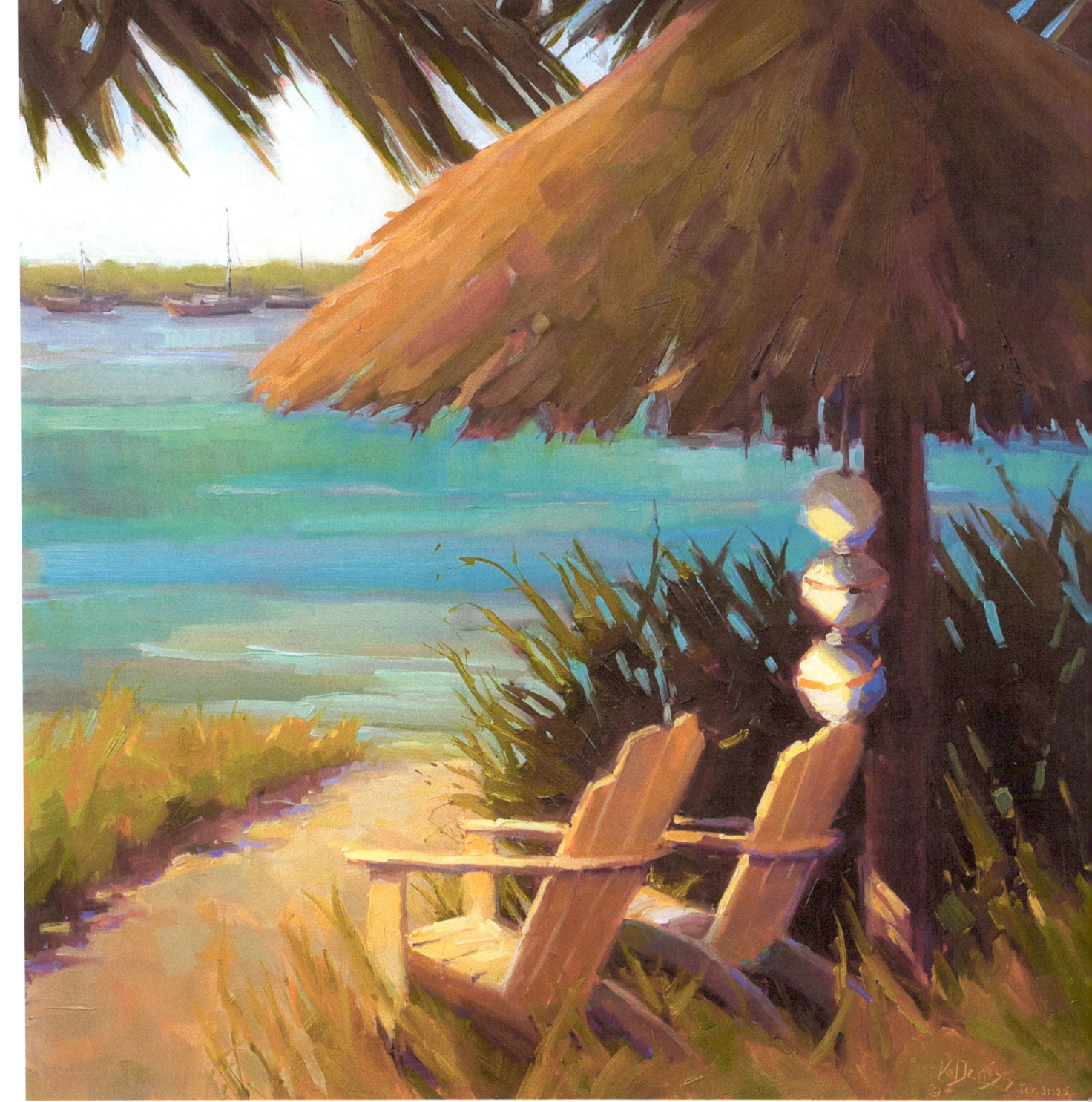

Kathleen Denis

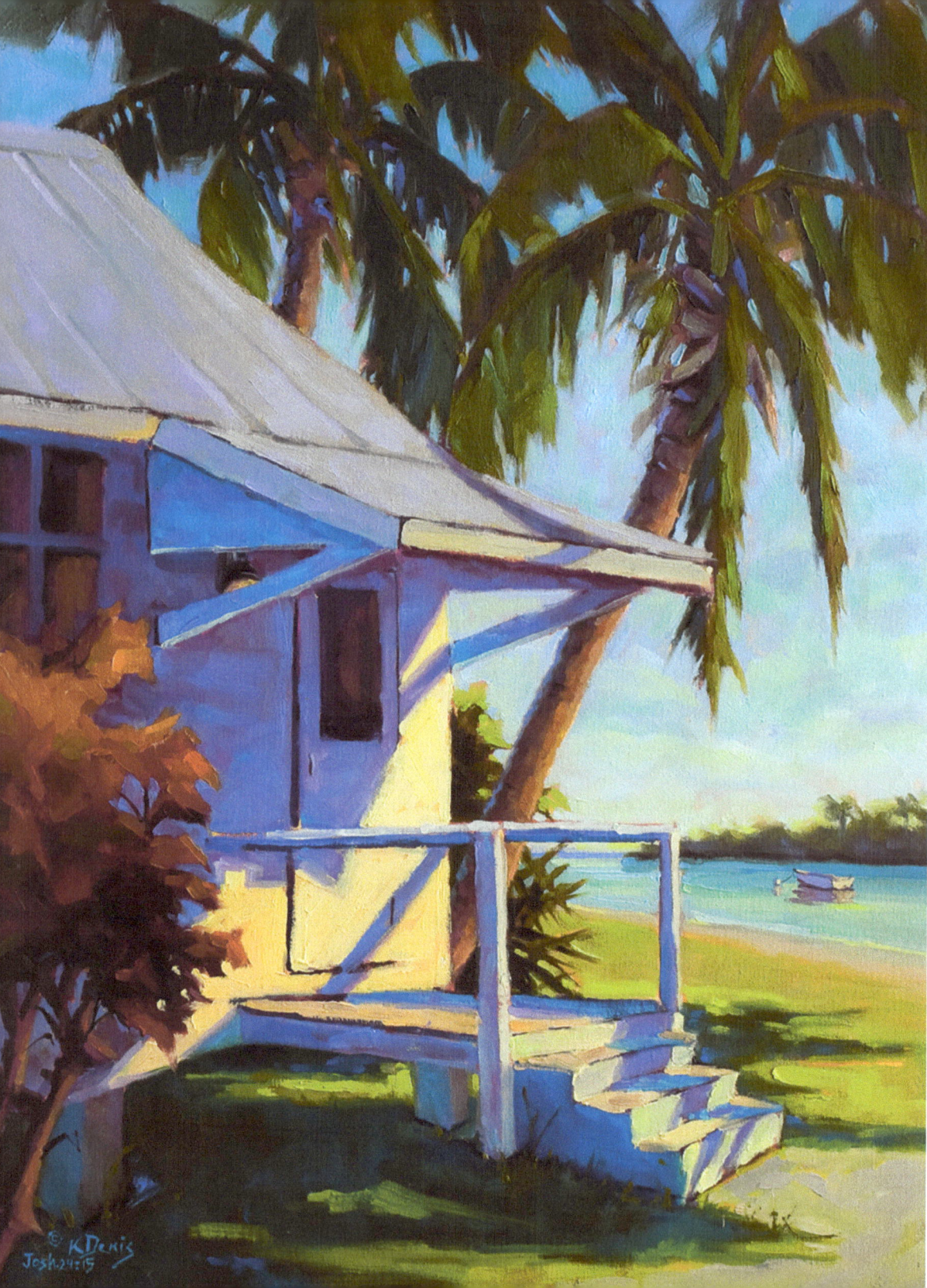

SATISFACTION GUARANTEED
24X18,
OIL ON PANEL

LOCATION:
PIGEON KEY,
MARATHON,
MILE MARKER 47

Painting or just visiting the historic Pigeon Key island is a step back in time you will not soon forget. I first painted there in 1995 as a student of Jeanne Dobie, a master watercolorist, and since returned many times as a participant in the annual Pigeon Key Art Festival. Most of the same buildings on the island are present today, but with many renovations, and are filled with interesting historical materials and photographs. This five-acre island, which may be visited by ferry boat, served as a home base for railroad workers constructing and later operating the final installment of Henry M. Flagler's Key West Extension of the Florida East Coast Railway: the Old Seven-Mile Bridge.

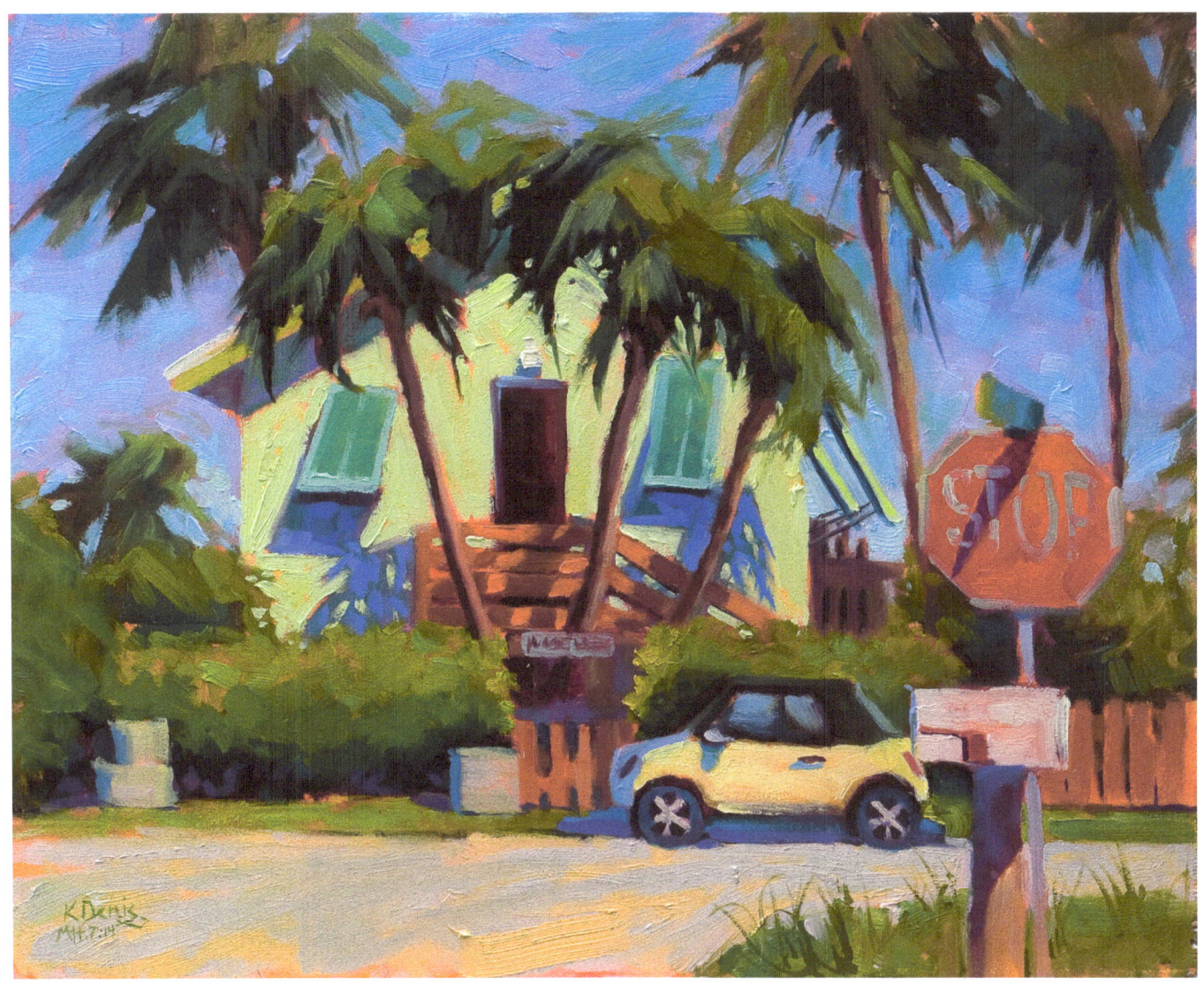

OFF THE HIGHWAY 11X14, OIL ON PANEL

LOCATION: IT'S A SECRET!

My painting friend, Priscilla Coote from Key West, invited me to paint with her at one of her favorite "secret" spots. And here's where I found this charming, old conch cottage *off the highway* between Islamorada and Key West.

Kathleen Denis

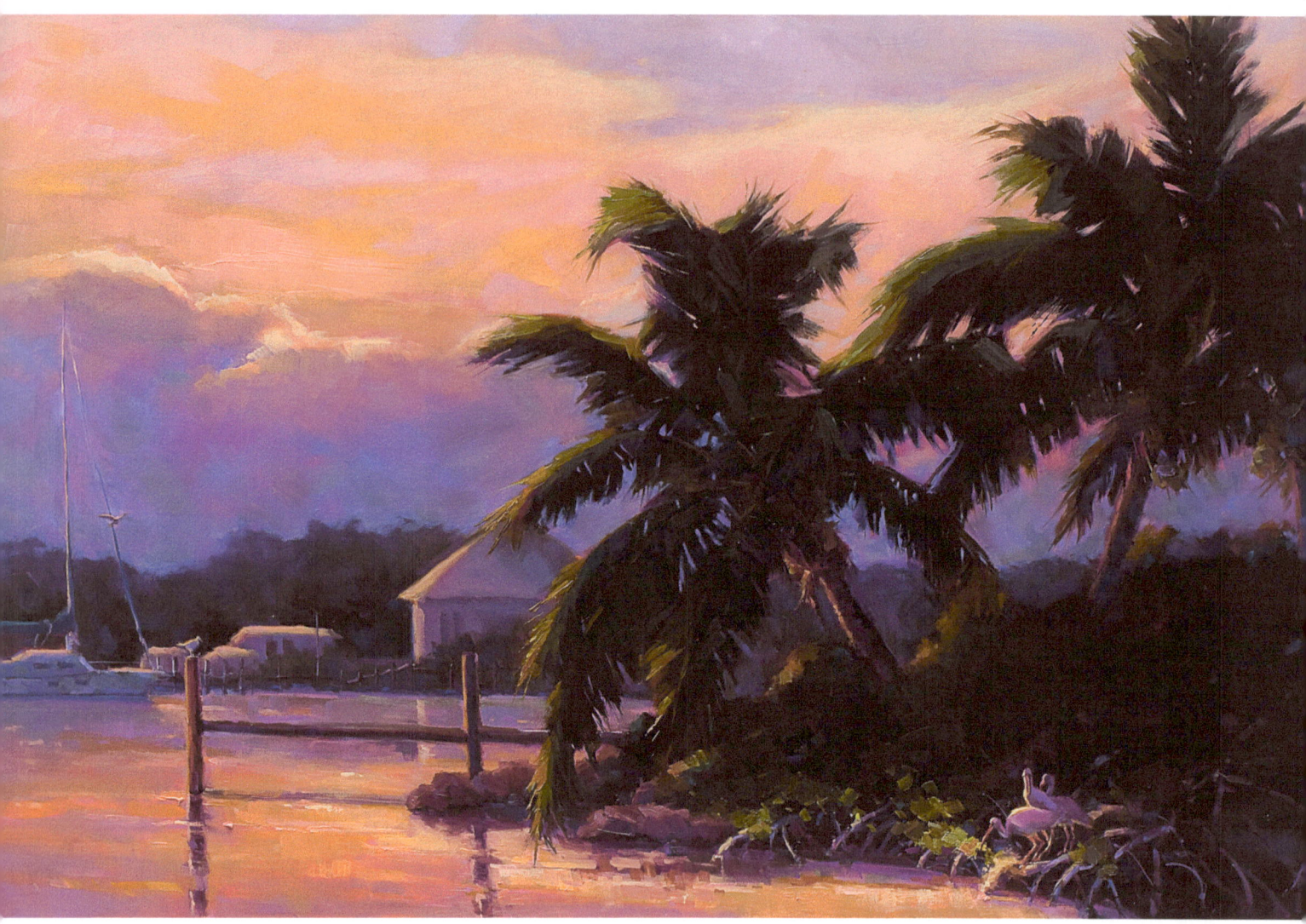

SUNSET CELEBRATION OIL ON CANVAS, 36X60

LOCATION: LOWER MATECUMBE, BAYSIDE

Where is the best place to see sunsets in the Florida Keys? Wherever the sun sets! No matter how many times I have the opportunity to see the sun going down, it's always breathtaking. Here in the Keys we have some of the most incredible sunsets to be found. Every night is a *celebration* painted by God!

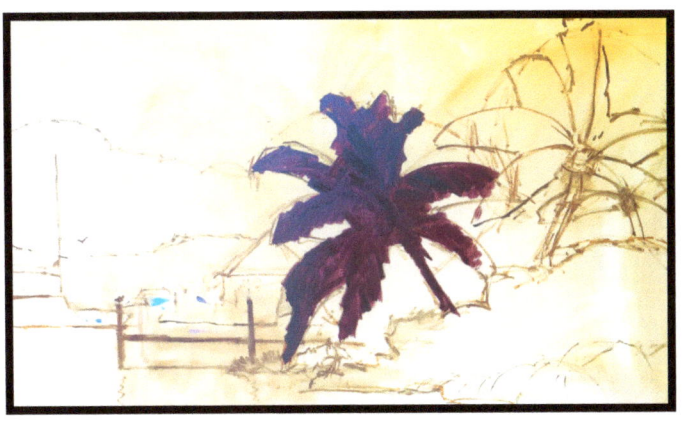

1. THE SKETCH

This is how I began. First I toned my canvas and then I laid in a loose sketch, both with a burnt umber color; different than my usual more saturated orange tones. Then I mixed up some colors, and as you can see, I tested them on the canvas in small spots. After that I began to block in the color of the tree shapes.

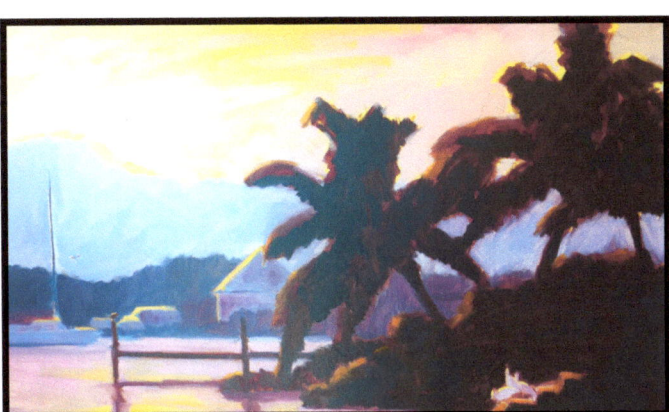

2. BLOCK IN COLORS

In this block in step I begin to divide my lights from my shadows and paint accordingly.

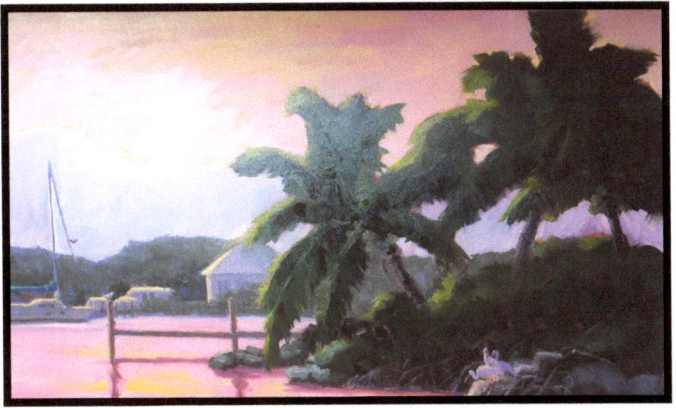

3. LAYING IN THE LOCAL COLORS

At this stage the objects begin to take on more of their true colors, while their form becomes more realistic. I continue developing, refining and detailing the painting until I feel it's completed.

Kathleen Denis

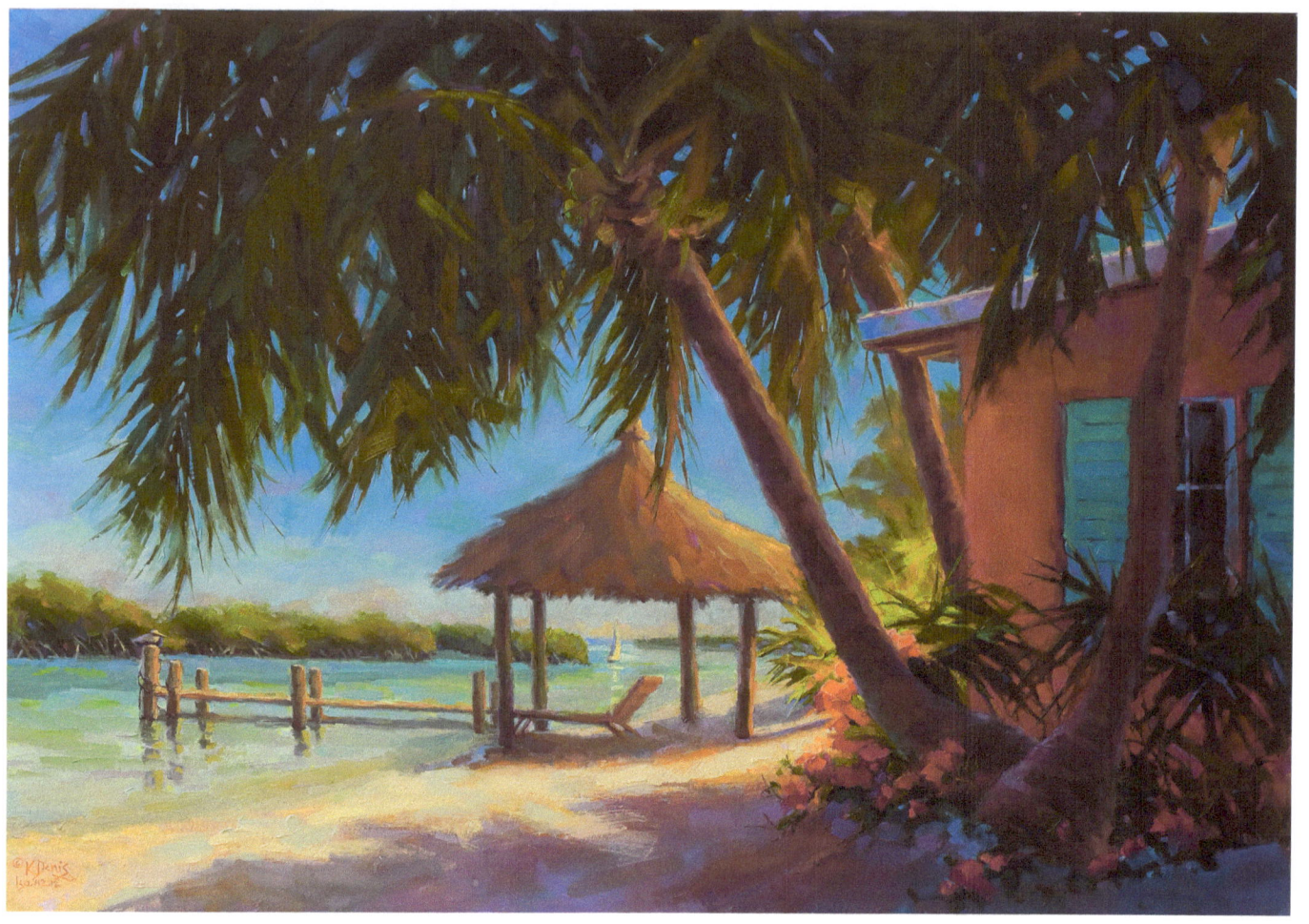

A DAY IN PARADISE 24X36, OIL ON PANEL

LOCATION: SUNSET COVE BEACH RESORT – 99360 OVERSEAS HIGHWAY, KEY LARGO

Painting at this mom-and-pop resort brings back childhood memories of the old charm that still remains. Tiki huts, transparent water, beachfront cottages, kayaks and hammocks: truly a day in paradise!

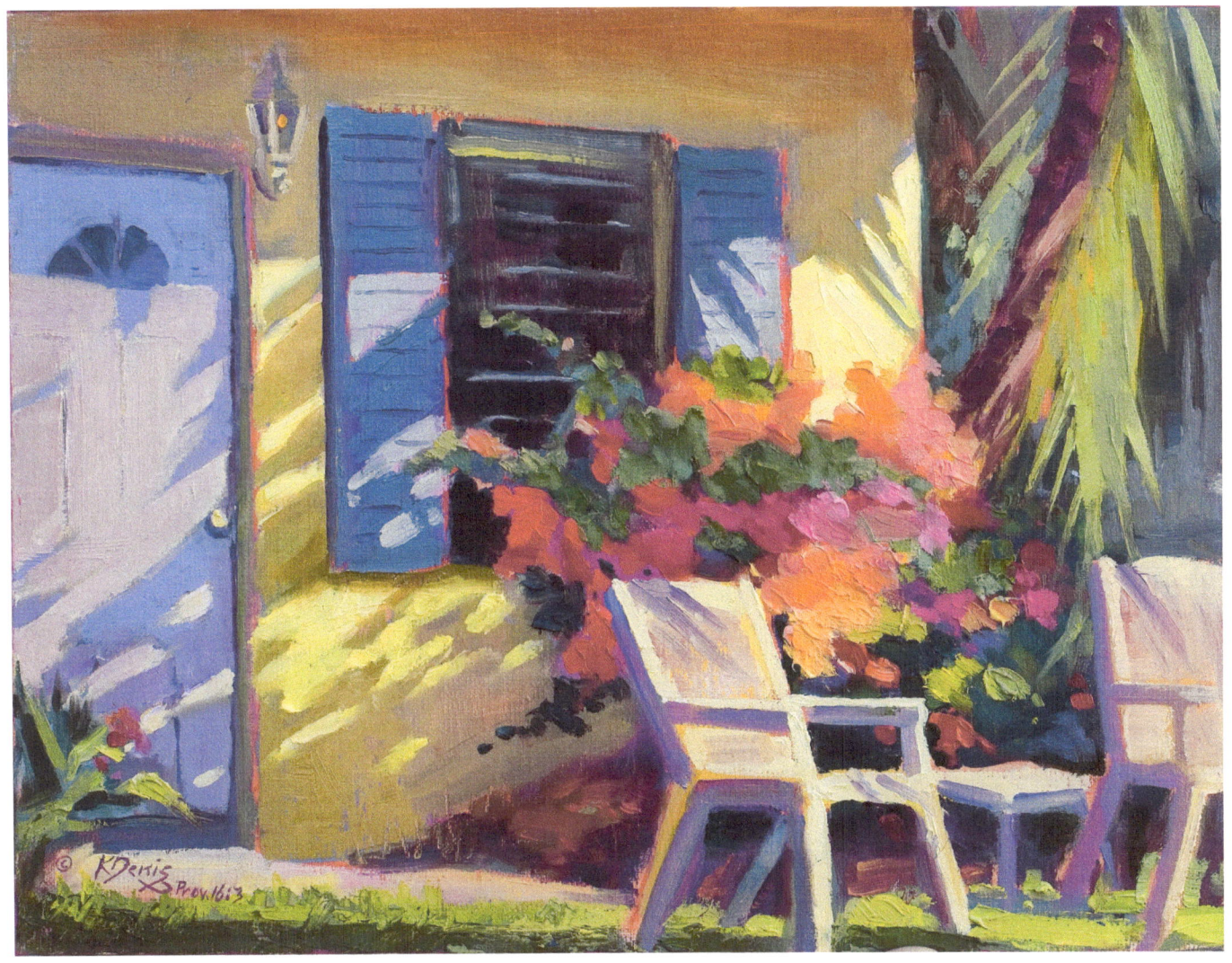

KEY LARGO MORNING 9X12, OIL ON LINEN

LOCATION: SUNSET COVE BEACH RESORT – 99360 OVERSEAS HIGHWAY, KEY LARGO

This painting won the Best of Show Ribbon at the "Art Guild of the Purple Isles" Annual Art Show 2012.

"Art Guild of the Purple Isles" serves an important role in the art community in the Upper Florida Keys. Established in 1966, with the goal to promote an interest in and an appreciation of art, sponsor educational opportunities for members and local schools, and host to art shows, plein air painting, workshops and social events, not to mention, it has some of the finest folks you could ever meet. www,purpleislesartguild.com.

Kathleen Denis

"If you hear a voice within you
which says 'you cannot paint,'
then by all means paint, and that
voice will be silenced."
–Vincent Van Gogh

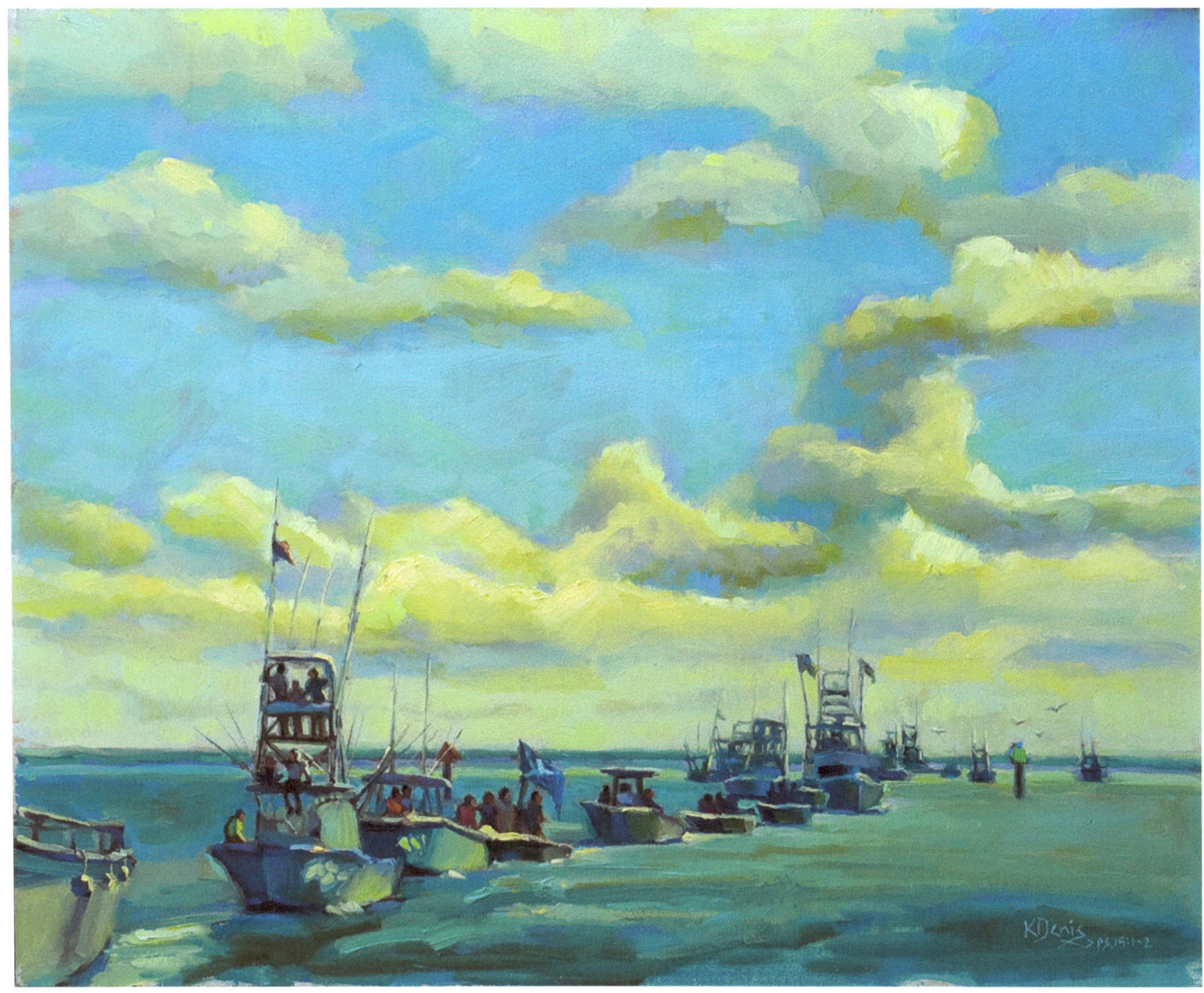

BLESSING OF THE FLEET 16X20, OIL ON PANEL

LOCATION: WHALE HARBOR BRIDGE AT MILE MARKER 83

This 43rd Annual *Blessing of the Fleet* is a Florida Keys tradition that takes place on New Year's morning in Islamorada at mile marker 83. Proceeding up the channel each boat is blessed in turn by various clergy standing on the Whale Harbor Bridge. Followed up by a BBQ at Whale Harbor Marina is a great way to bring in the New Year!

Kathleen Denis

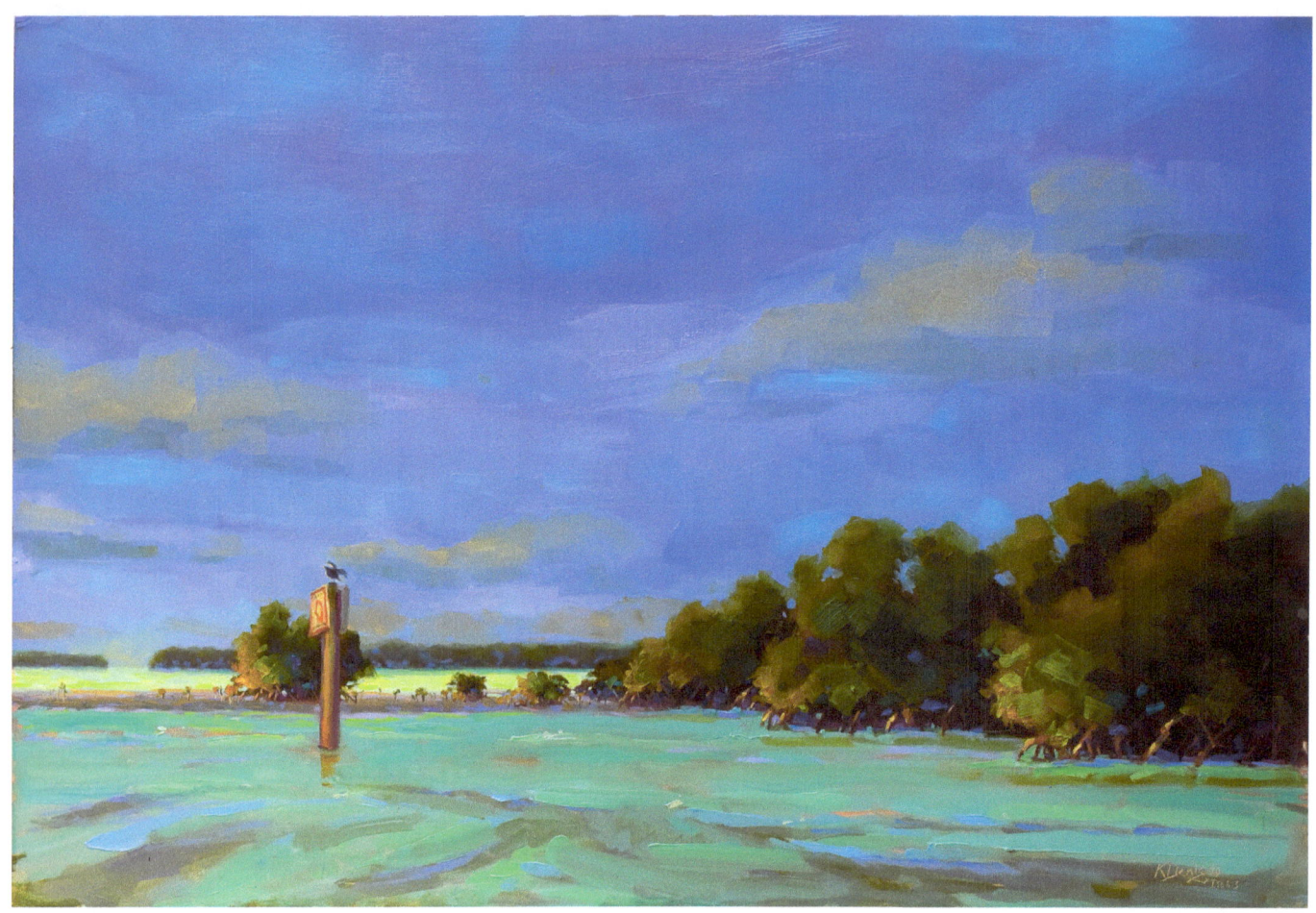

INCOMING TIDE 24X36, OIL ON PANEL

Paddle boarding to this bayside view, not far from my house, is always a favorite place to find scenes to paint. Seeing fish and other underwater life through the clear waters, especially manatee and dolphin, never gets old.

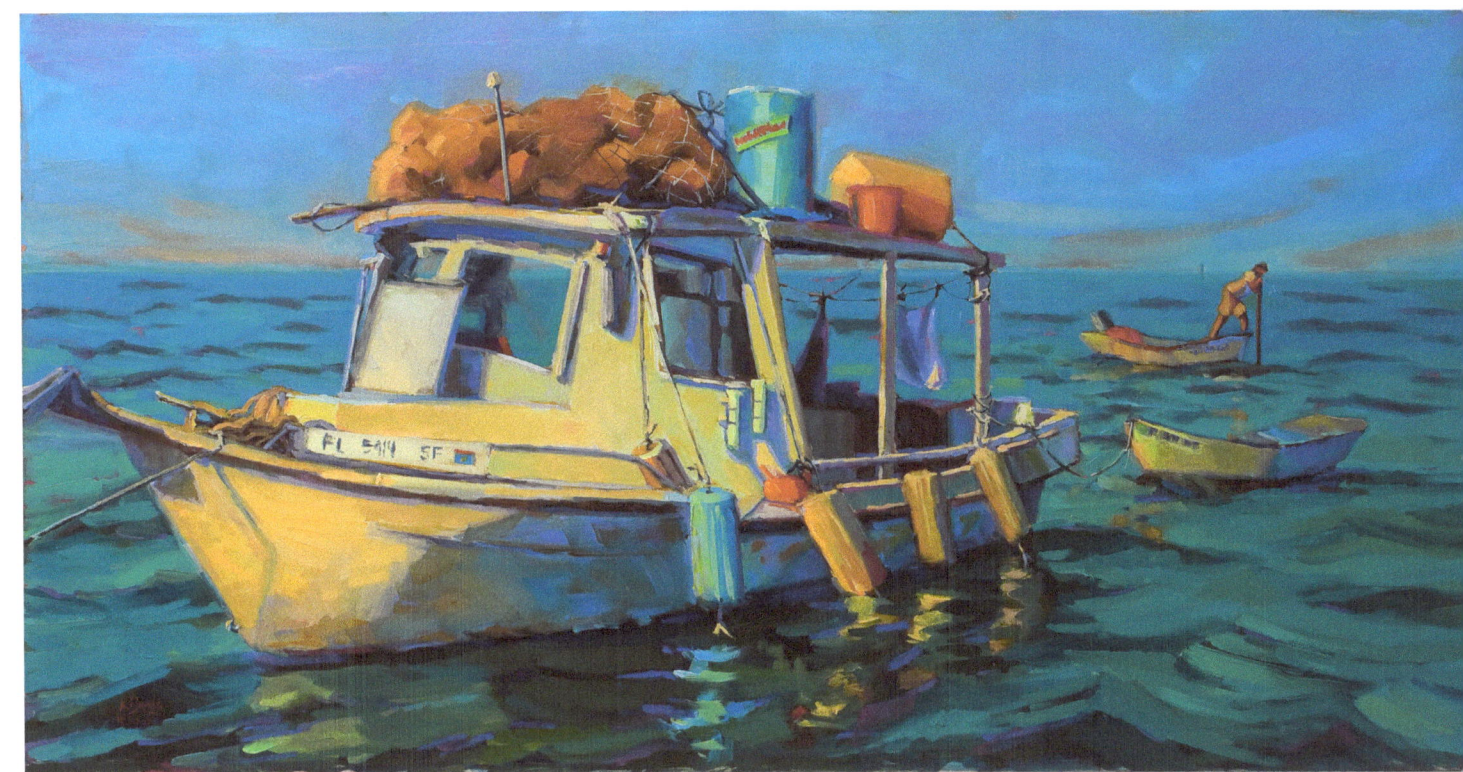

SPONGEBOB SPONGE BOAT 18X36, OIL ON PANEL

LOCATION: THE FLORIDA BAY, ISLAMORADA

Pirates, Indians and sponges were common creatures in the Florida Keys at one time. While a deadly sponge fungus destroyed most of the beds around the Florida Keys, the last twenty-five years have seen a restoration allowing several small businesses to harvest Keys sponges today.

Diving for sponges in the Keys is prohibited now, so fishermen, commonly known as "hookers," harvest sponges by using a hook on a long pole to tear a sponge free from the bottom. They often work from small boats, with a larger "mother" ship close by. I felt privileged to have seen this "hooker" hard at work and to be able to capture on canvas this almost lost occupation.

Kathleen Denis

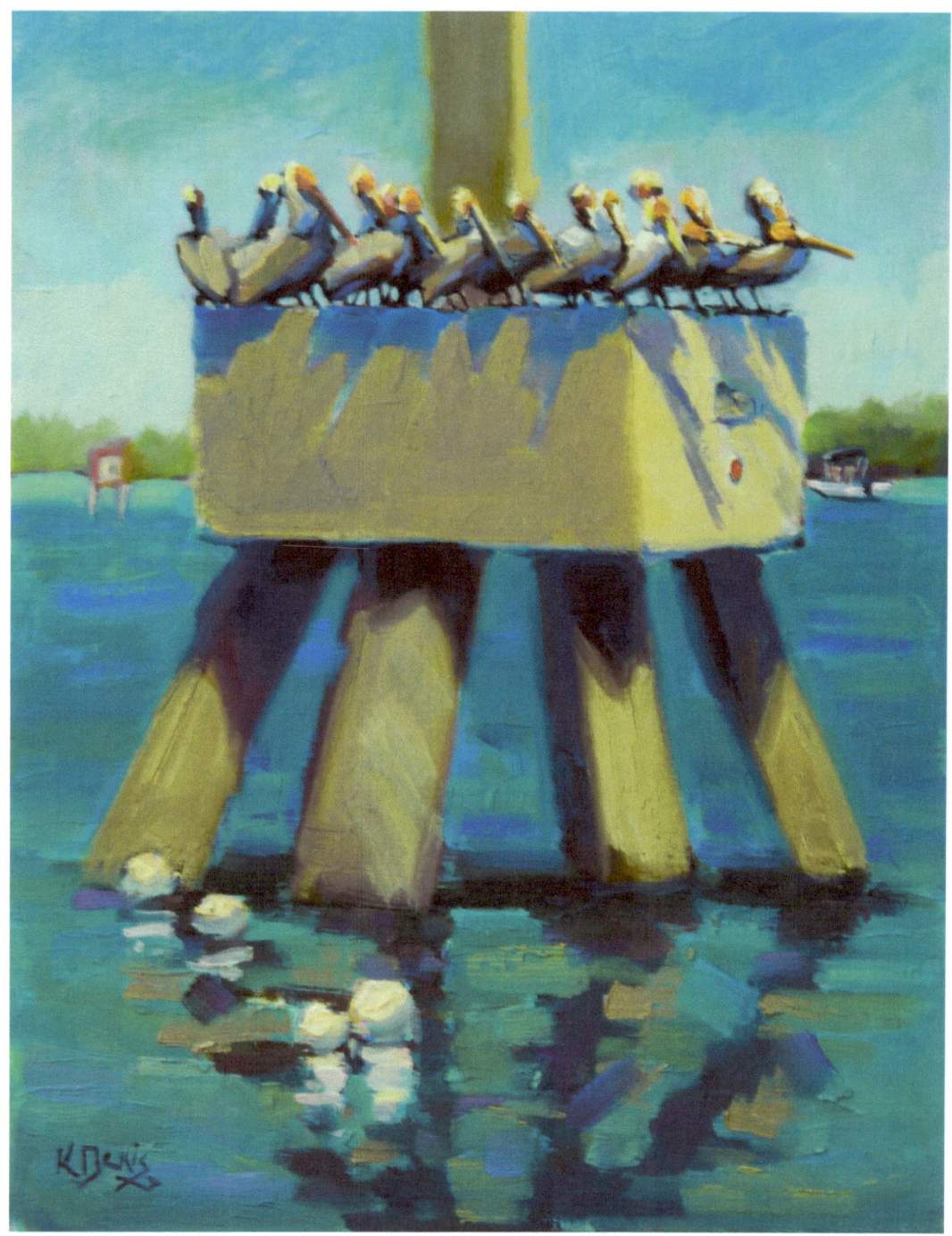

KEYS CONVENTION
1OX8, OIL ON PANEL

LOCATION:
FLORIDA KEYS

I spotted this gathering of pelicans on our way out to sea. Perhaps they are discussing fishing strategies for the day? Who knows!

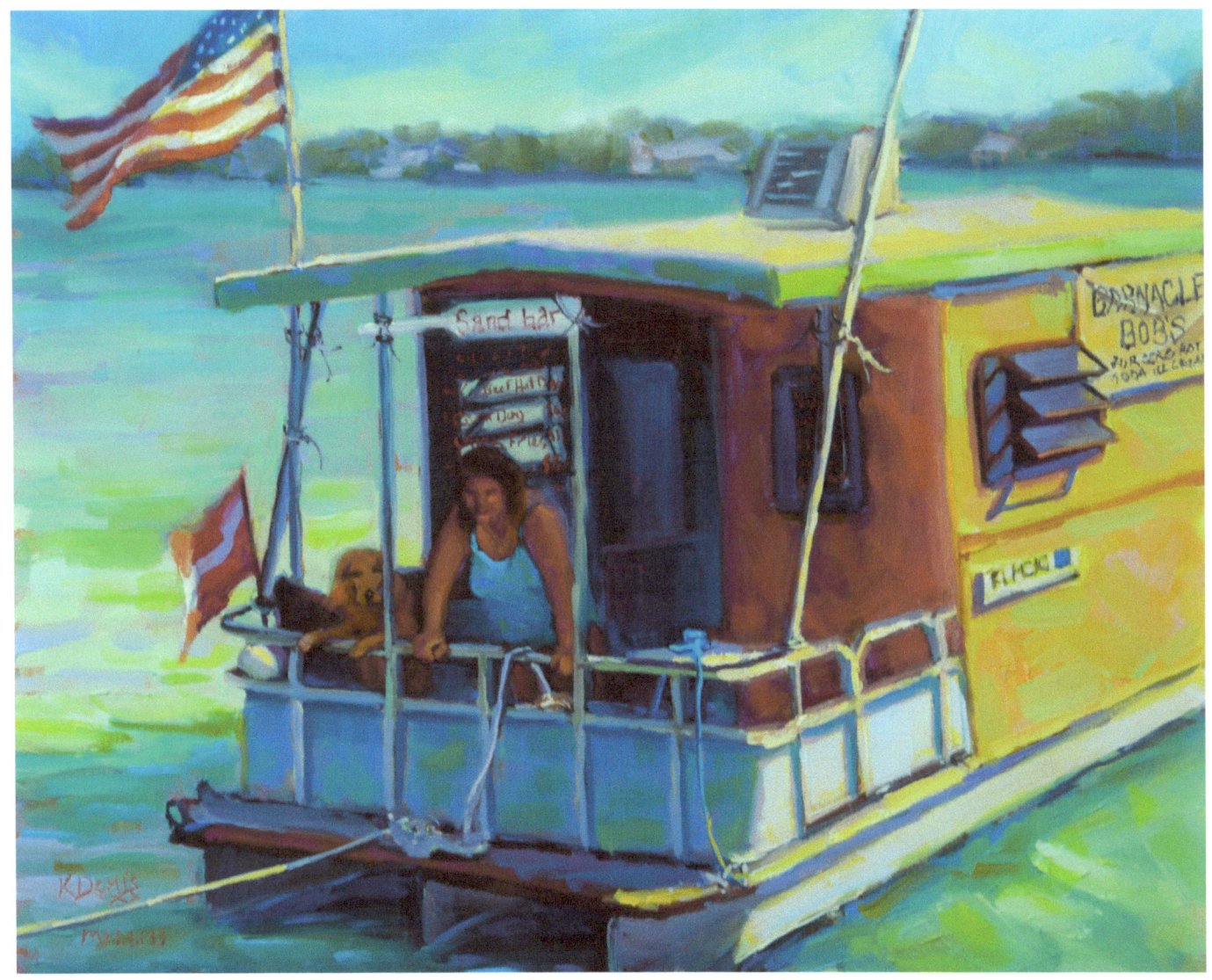

BARNACLE BOB'S TAKE OUT 11X14, OIL ON PANEL

LOCATION: SANDBAR AT MILE MARKER 84

This popular icon on the Whale Harbor Channel sandbar fills the air with delicious smells of burgers, chicken and fries. A "must have" to keep the day going.

Kathleen Denis

PAINTING PARADISE: The Florida Keys
Past Memories & Present Moments

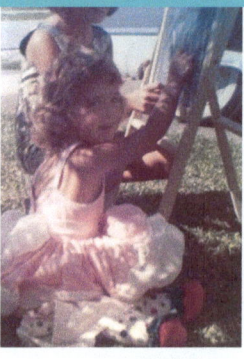

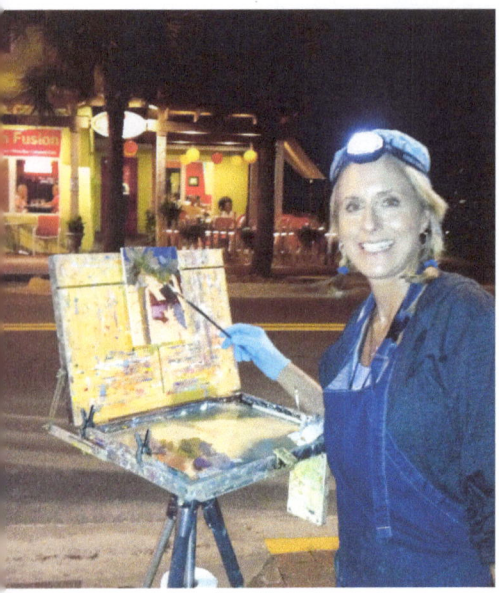

The Florida Keys captured my heart at a very young age. Having grown up in South Florida, it was one of my family's favorite vacation spots. Fishing, diving and watching sunsets were included in frequent trips with our boat and camper in tow. Driving on the Overseas Highway, surrounded by the open sea and sky, formed many fond memories for me.

As times change, so do some of the places our memories consist of. The charm of old rustic buildings and mom and pop motels, have through the years, often given way to more modern establishments. I recall gas stations being closed on Sundays, necessitating Saturday fill-ups in order to make it back to the mainland. My dad's favorite restaurant, The Coral Grill, encompassed an enormous buffet with every kind of seafood imaginable; sadly, it's no longer there.

[TOP]
Nocturnal Painting
Painting at night is always an exciting challenge.

[TOP]
Where it all began
Having fun with art at an early age came natural for me. At age four, my parents enrolled me in art classes, and because of that I often encourage parents to get their children art lessons early on if they show an interest. You never know...there may be an artist hiding within.

[LEFT] **Teaching Workshops & Classes**
I enjoy sharing my artistic knowledge, while watching others develop their talents further.

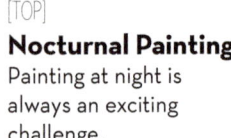

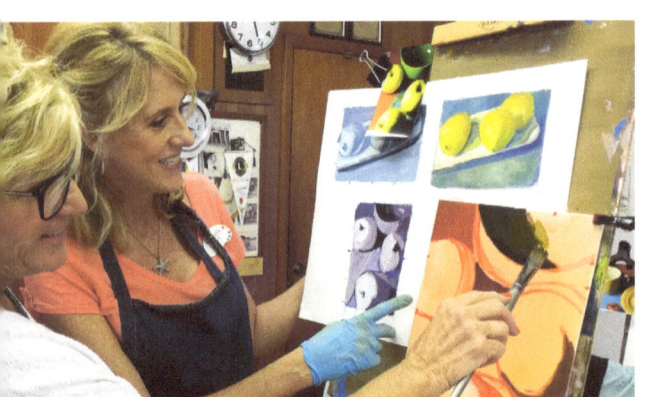

With progress comes the inevitable closing of some favorite places once enjoyed. As an artist, choosing to paint the Keys scenery was an easy decision. Returning to paradise, the place where warmhearted memories began, now holds an even greater splendor. The colors are more vivid and breathtaking than what I remember. Majestic swaying palm trees, glowing bougainvillea, the never ending quest for snapper and lobster, scrumptious Key lime pies, and the most peaceful color of water imaginable all serve to inspire creativity. To this day, aquamarine remains my favorite and most frequently used palette color.

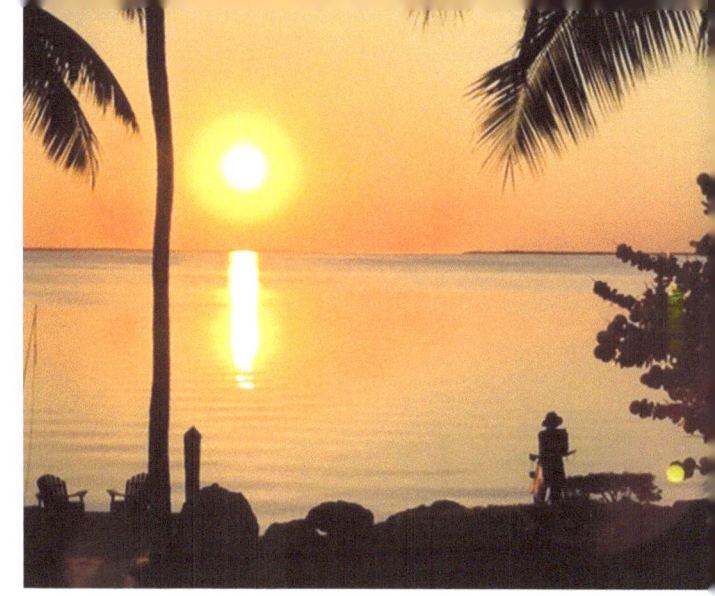

Dreams do not only come true in fairy tales. Over the years, I often thought how fabulous it would be to someday live in the Keys. That "someday" has arrived as my husband Jeff and I now live in paradise, along with our three Yorkshire terriers, Barney, Ruby and Callie. As a Pastor, Jeff felt called to establish a church here with a desire to help those in need, and I now enjoy my two greatest longings—painting paradise and ministering hope to other island residents. My passion is to capture and preserve on canvas, the extraordinary beauty and unusual charm of the Florida Keys that, with time, may not exist due to destructive weather or predictable development. My desire with this book is for you to appreciate the sights and scenes located in the Keys, and to inspire within you a continuous love for these islands, as well as a longing to create fond memories of your own in paradise. I hope you enjoy my art and this book as much as I have enjoyed creating it. Please venture into each scene and imagine being there!

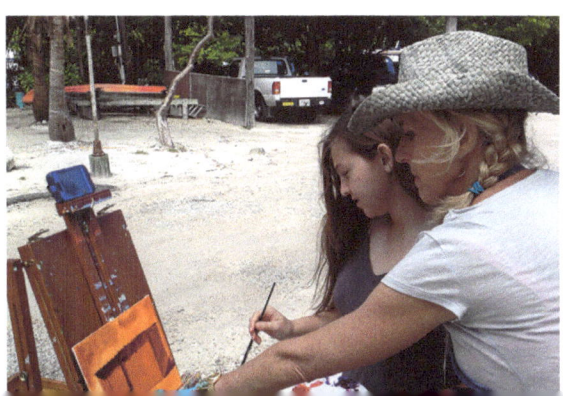

Kathleen Denis

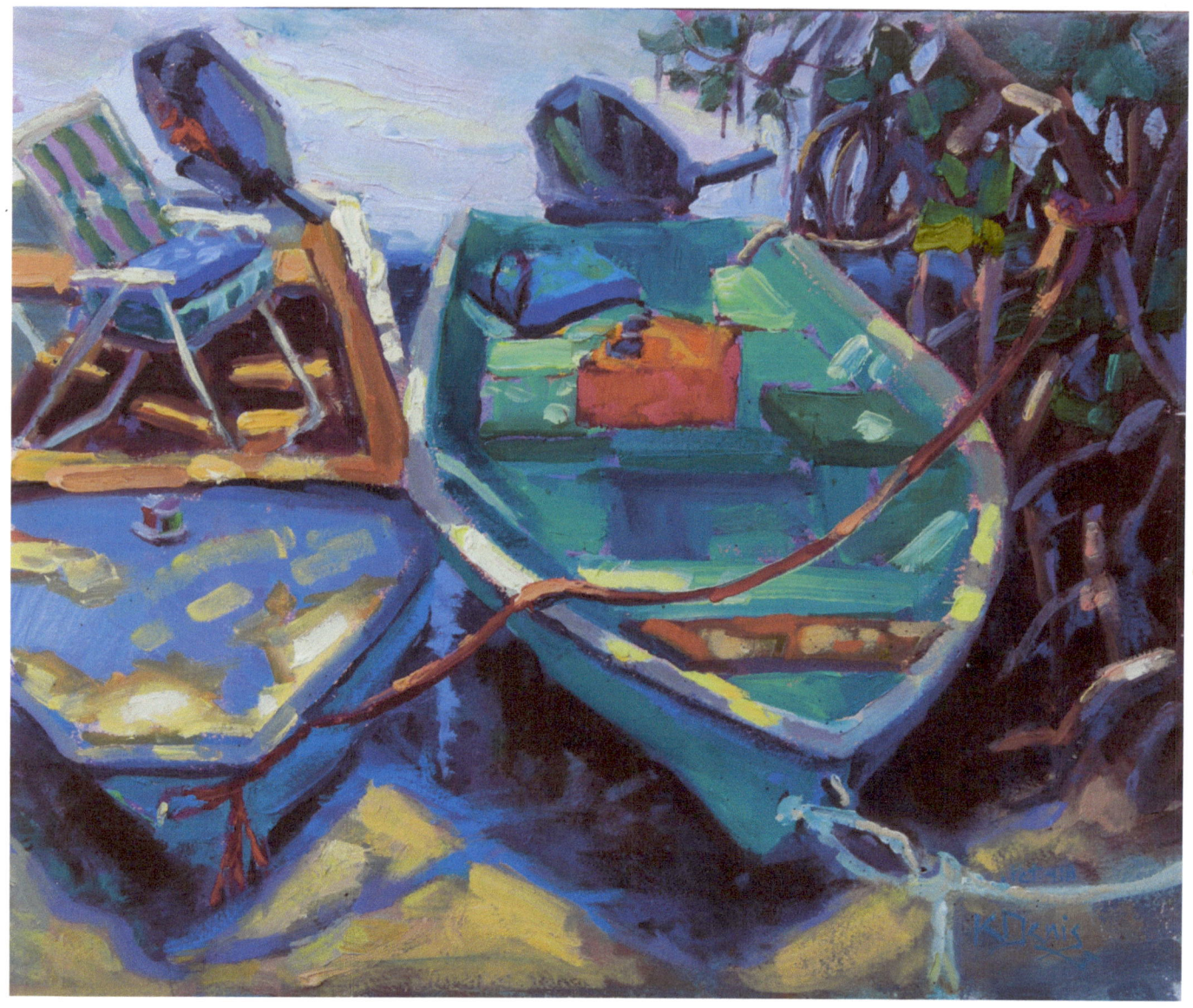

TOGETHER AGAIN 8X10, OIL ON PANEL

LOCATION: BLACKWOOD DRIVE, ISLAMORADA, MILE MARKER 81

A common scene in the Florida Keys is a ramp filled with colorful and unique dinghies. While their owners came to shore to work, replenish supplies or just get relief from a rocking boat, I painted their delightful means of transportation.

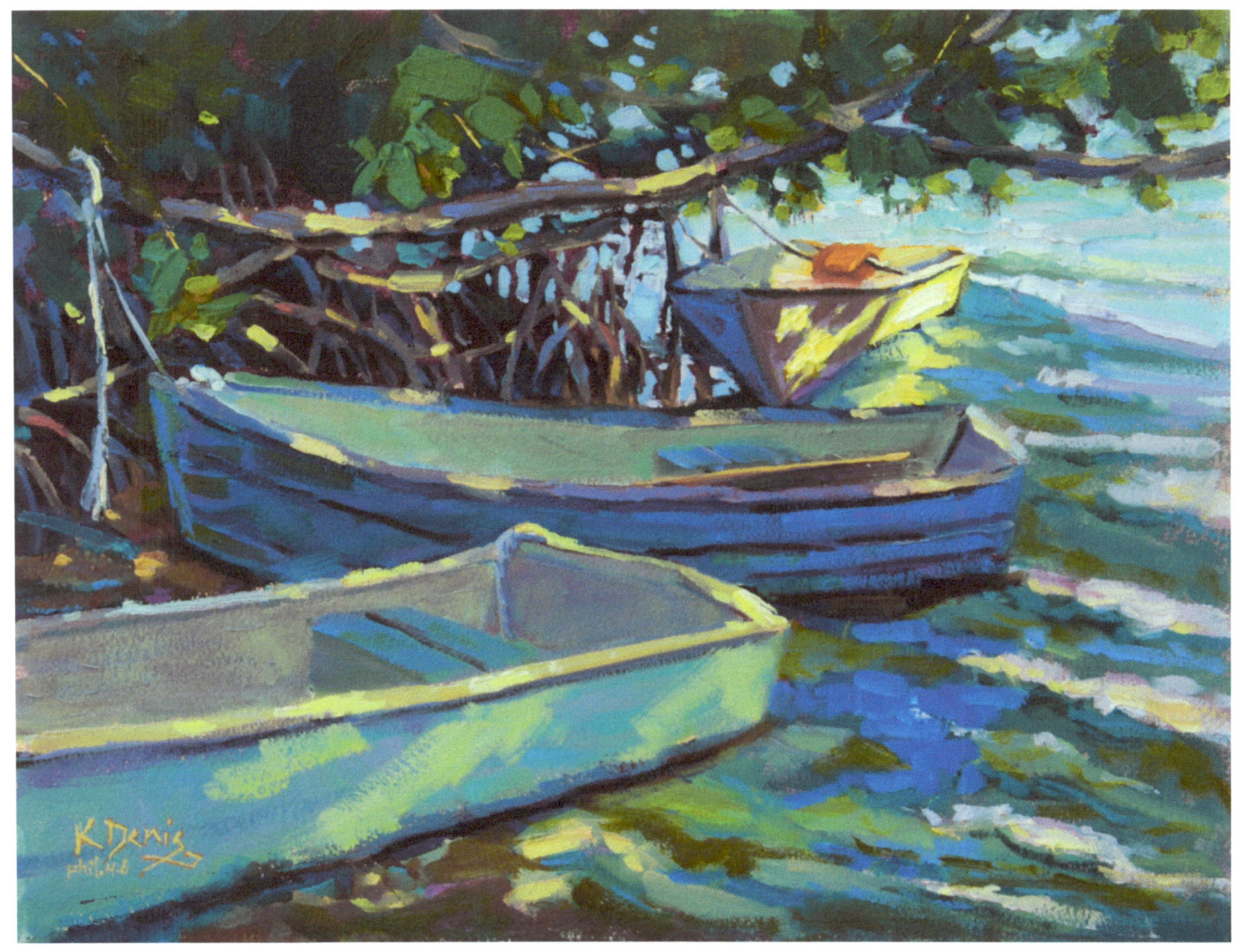

DEPARTMENT OF TRANSPORTATION 9X12, OIL ON PANEL

LOCATION: BLACKWOOD DRIVE, ISLAMORADA, MILE MARKER 81

Kathleen Denis

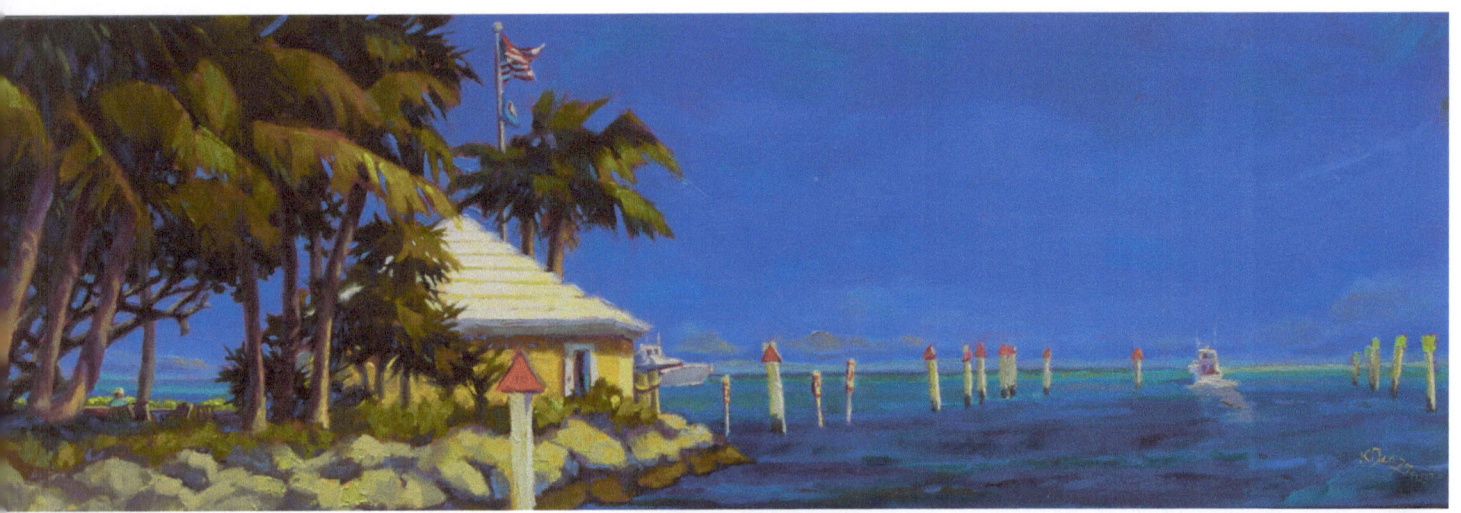

RED, RIGHT, RETURN
12X36, OIL ON CANVAS

LOCATION: OCEAN REEF CLUB,
KEY LARGO

Private, exclusive, unique are but a few words that describe this amazing gated town and club. Within this 2500 acres lies everything imaginable: golf, tennis, marina, wildlife, hotel, school, airport, restaurants, shops, hospital, theater, and art league.

During the seasonal months of November through March, I have the honor of teaching the intermediate/advanced oil and acrylic painting classes at the Ocean Reef Art League, one of my art career highlights!

[RIGHT] **THE OPENING** 9X12, OIL ON PANEL

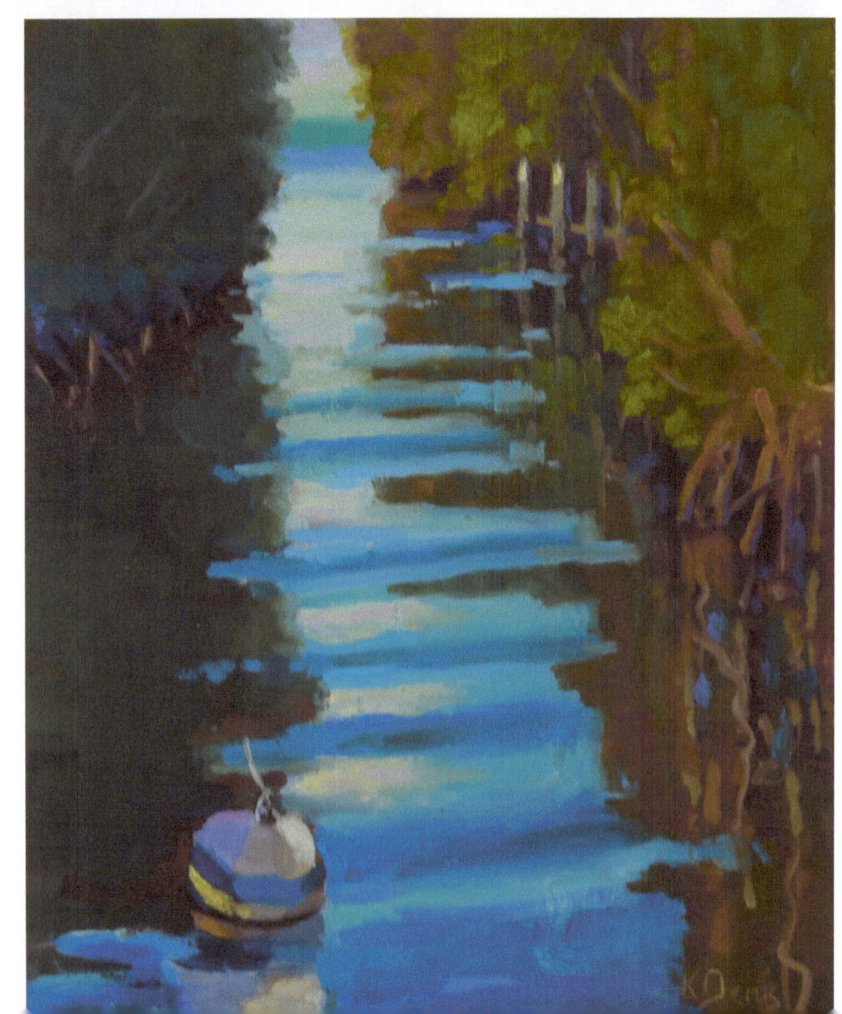

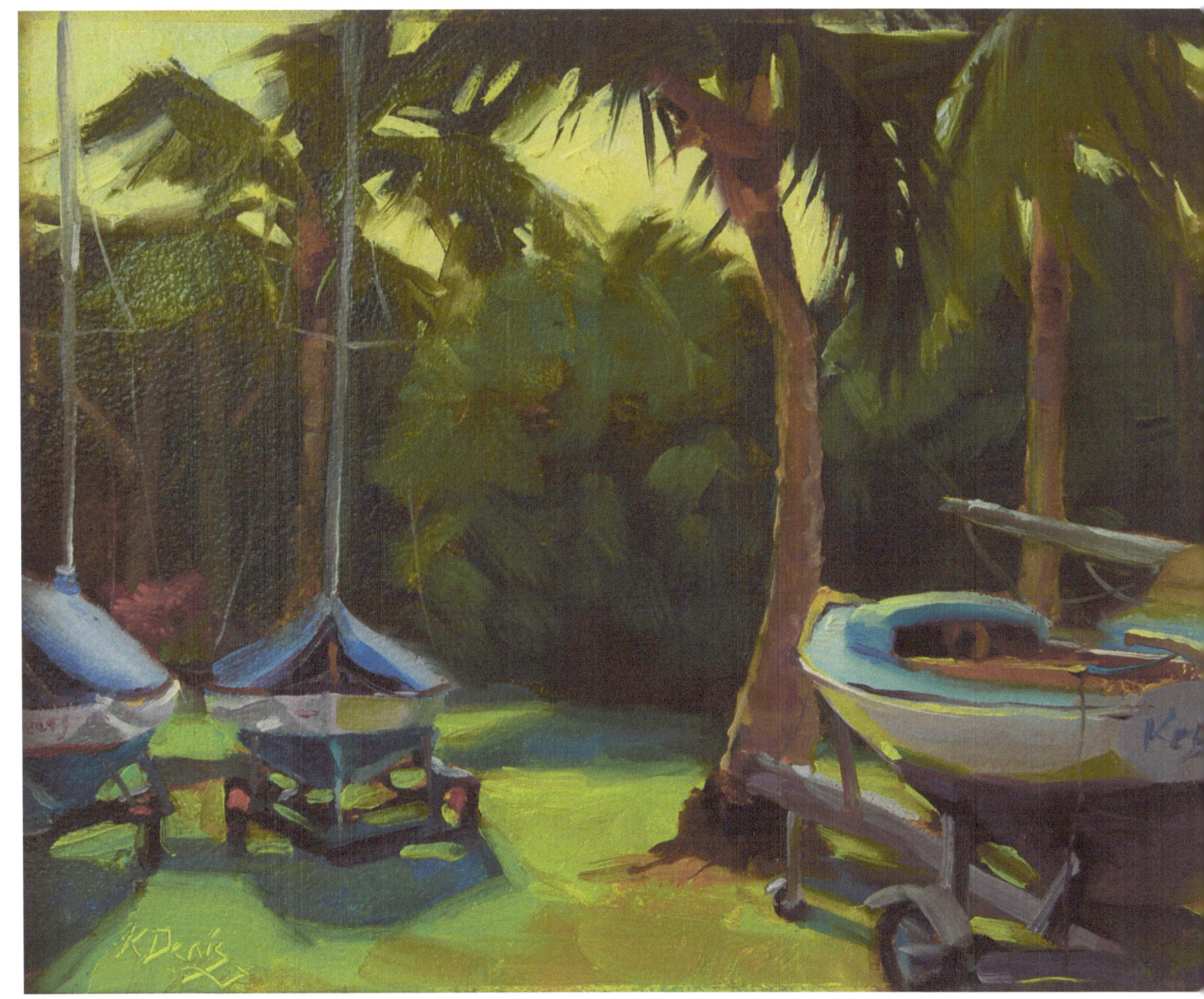

BAKER HARBOR 9X12, OIL ON PANEL

Kathleen Denis

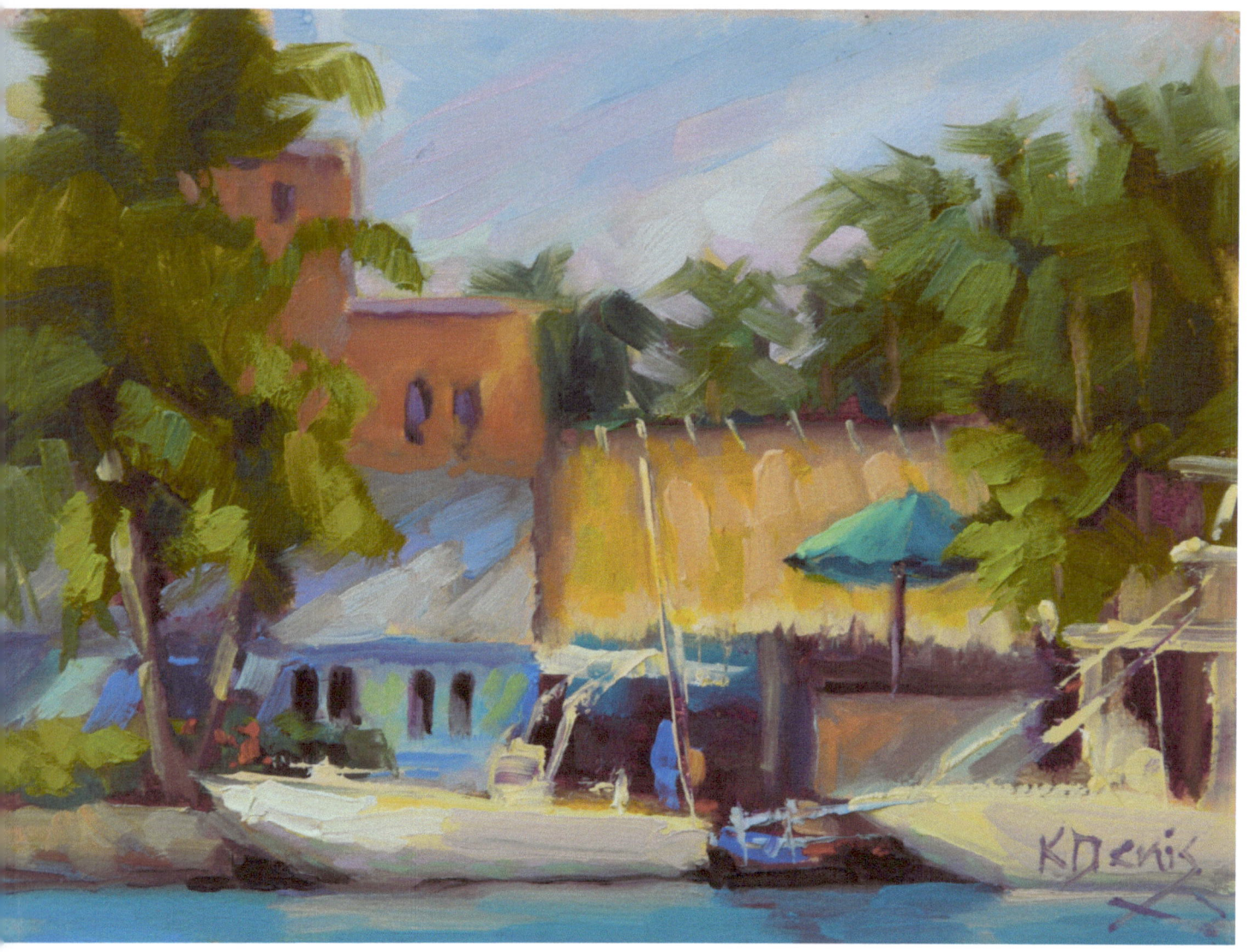

ACROSS THE WAY 5X7, OIL ON PANEL

LOCATION: HAMMER POINT, TAVERNIER

Boats, tiki huts, palm trees and hammocks: the most common backyard scene *across the way* from waterfront homes in the Keys.

**BEYOND THE
CLOUDS**
6X6,
OIL ON PANEL

LOCATION:
MOMMA
LEE'S HOME,
HAMMER POINT,
TAVERNIER

There are some people who touch our lives in such a way that will never be forgotten and Mama Lee was one of them. As I paint this, with love in my heart for her and her family from the backyard of where she once called home, I reflect on her "New Home" beyond the clouds.

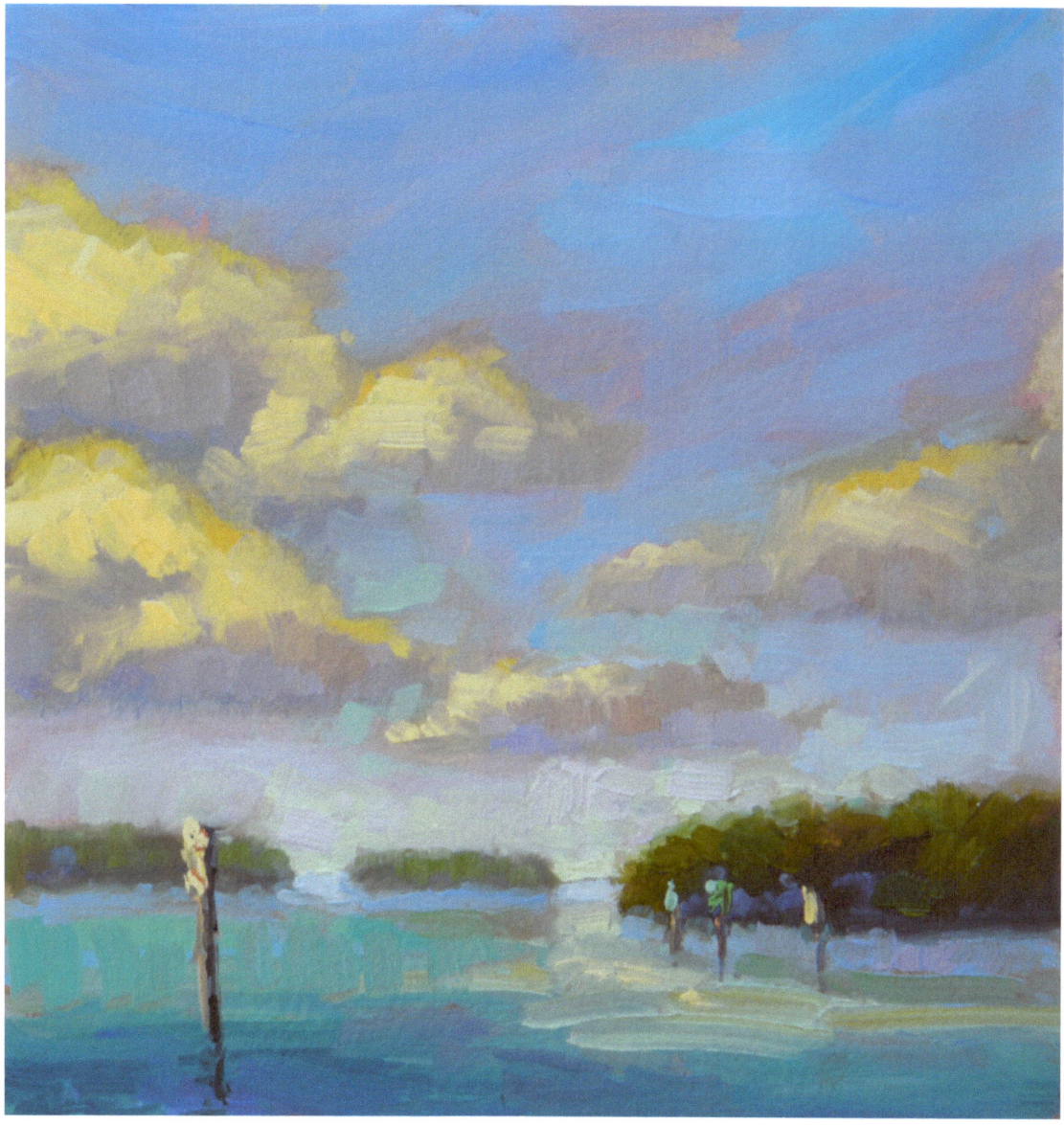

Kathleen Denis

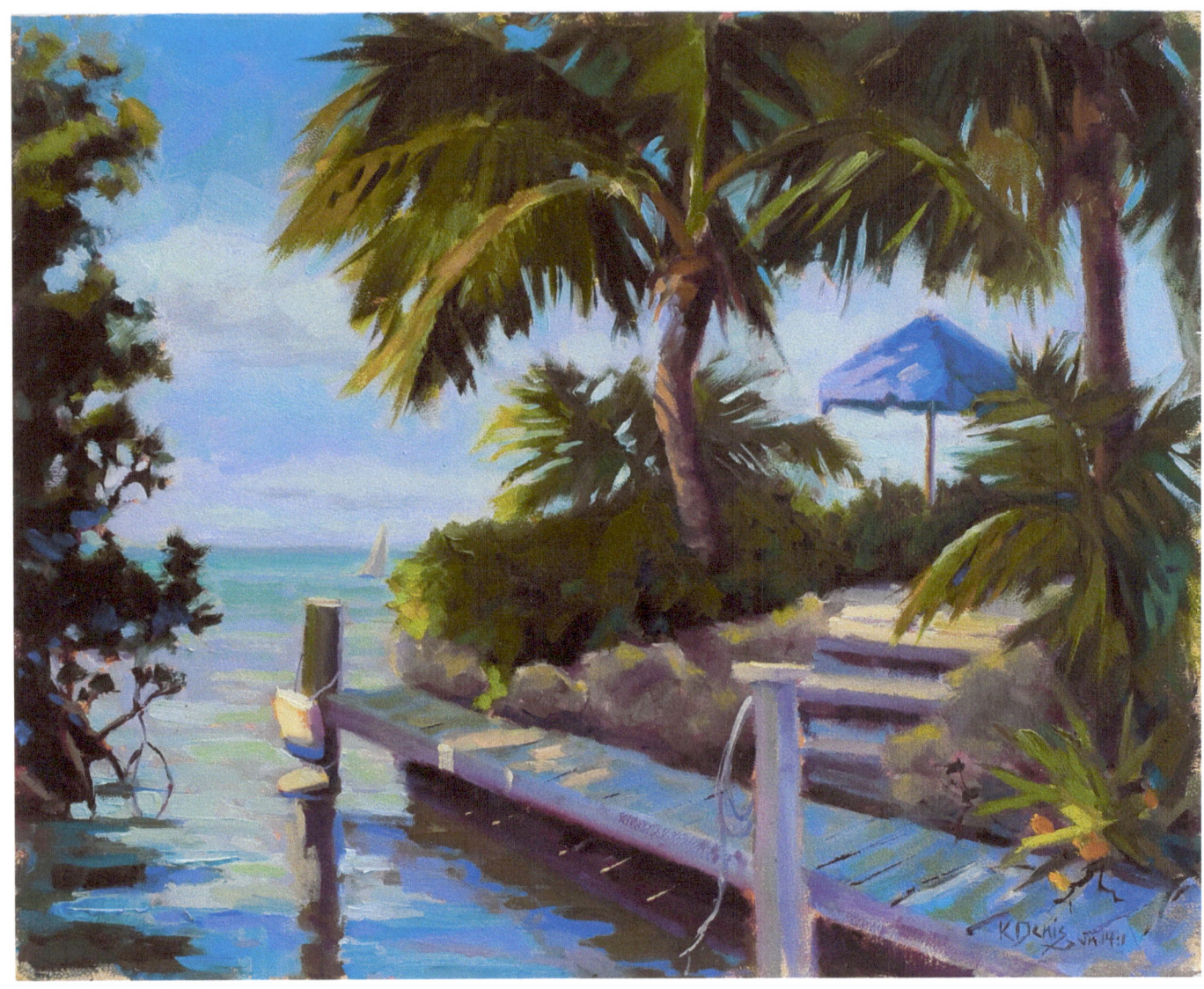

NO COMPLAINTS 11X14, OIL ON PANEL

LOCATION: JOHN AND LINDA VLAD'S HOME, ISLAMORADA

It doesn't get much better than this extraordinary hidden treasure located on the Florida Bay that John and Linda so kindly allowed me to capture on canvas. For over 20 years, they have been expanding the architecture in such a way that preserves the natural Keys hammock, allowing them to continually enjoy the outdoors. I would have *no complaints* living there!

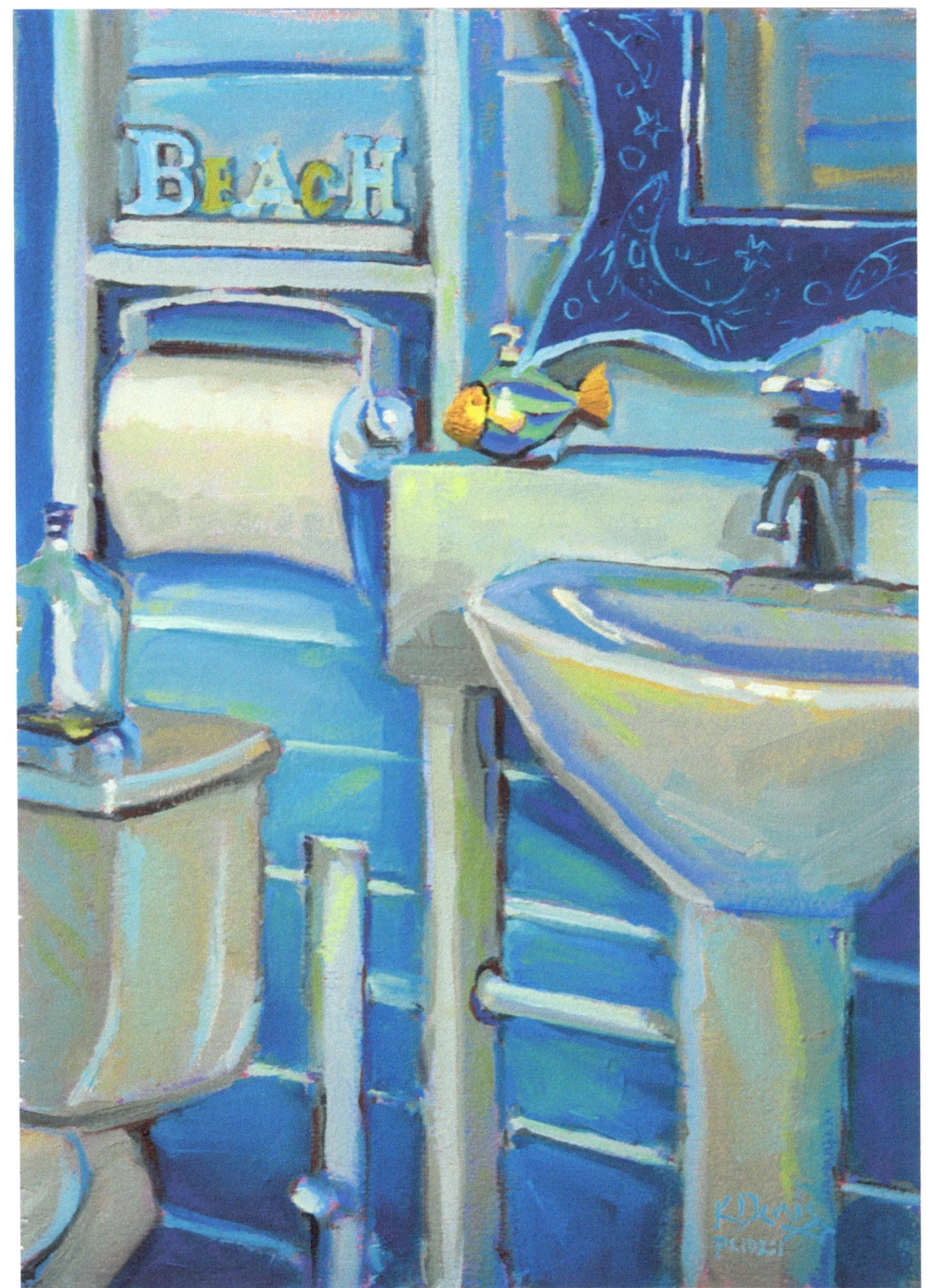

NECESSITIES
12X9, OIL ON PANEL

LOCATION: JOHN AND LINDA VLAD'S HOME, ISLAMORADA

There are some necessities in life, and one of them, if you live in the Keys, is a "Keysie" style bathroom.

This cabana bath is a natural for John and Linda's backyard that says "tropical dream house" everywhere you look.

Kathleen Denis

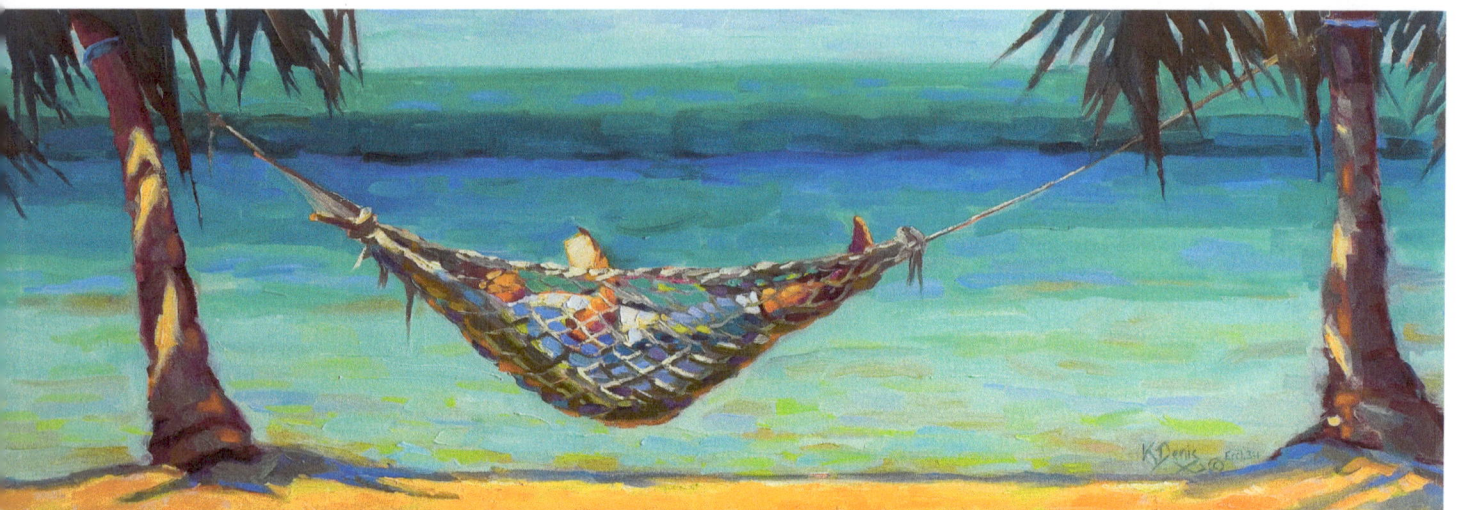

SICK DAY 12X36, OIL ON CANVAS

LOCATION: FOUNDERS PARK, 86800 OVERSEAS HIGHWAY, ISLAMORADA

Founders Park is one of my favorite places in Islamorada. It is home to several festivals, Olympic pool, doggie park, baseball fields, marina, tennis courts and beach, and offers something for almost everyone, including artists.

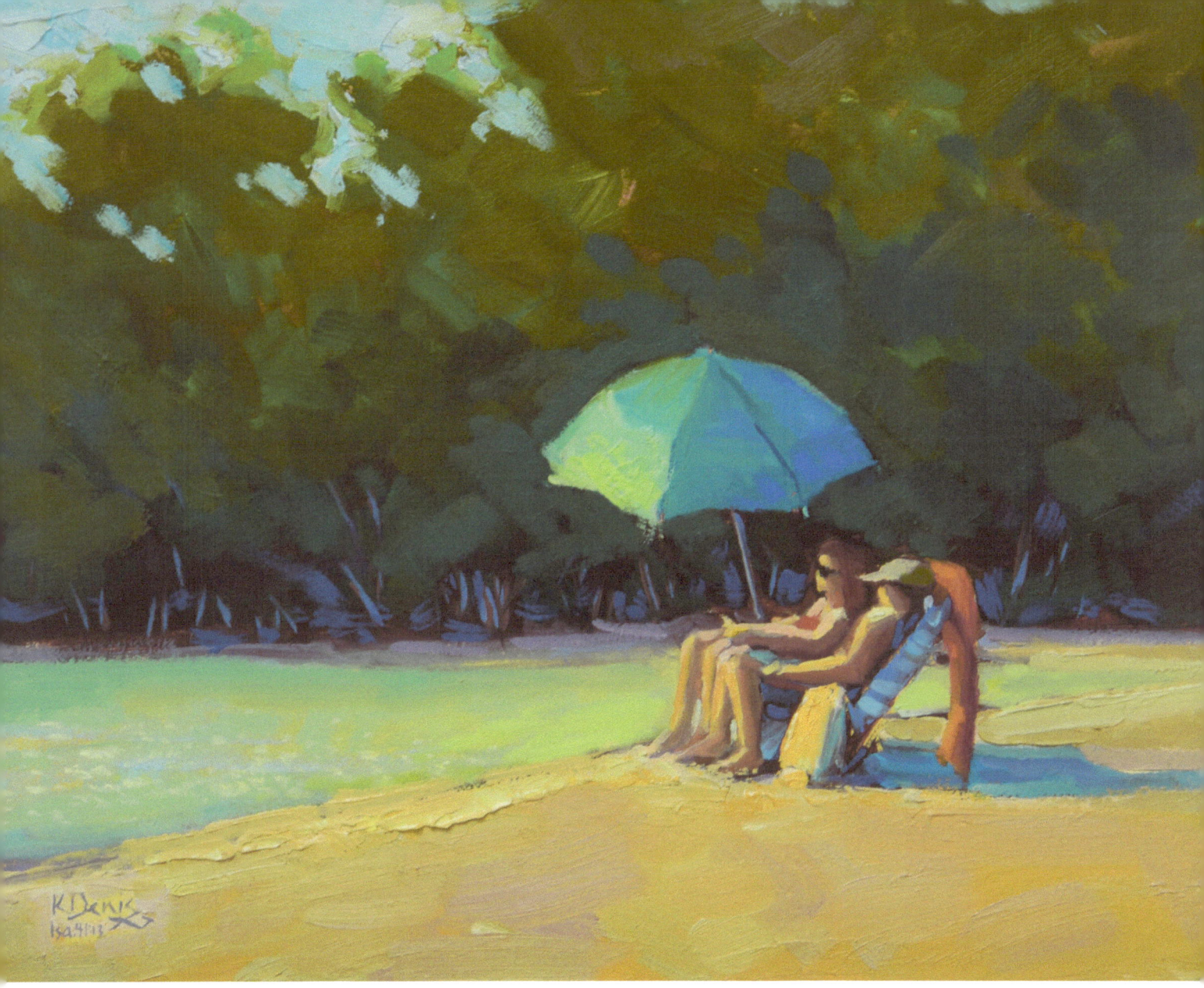

PLAY DAY 9X12, OIL ON PANEL

LOCATION: FOUNDERS PARK, 86800 OVERSEAS HIGHWAY, ISLAMORADA

Kathleen Denis

"Many believe–and I believe–
that I have been designated for
this work by God. In spite of my
old age, I do not want to give it
up; I work out of love for God
and I put all my hope in Him."
—Michelangelo

UNDER COVER
14X16,
OIL ON PANEL

LOCATION:
Drop Anchor
Resort and
Marina,
84959 Overseas
Highway,
Islamorada

Both colorful
architecture
and easy-going
cats, which are
plentiful in the
Florida Keys,
beckon me to
paint them.

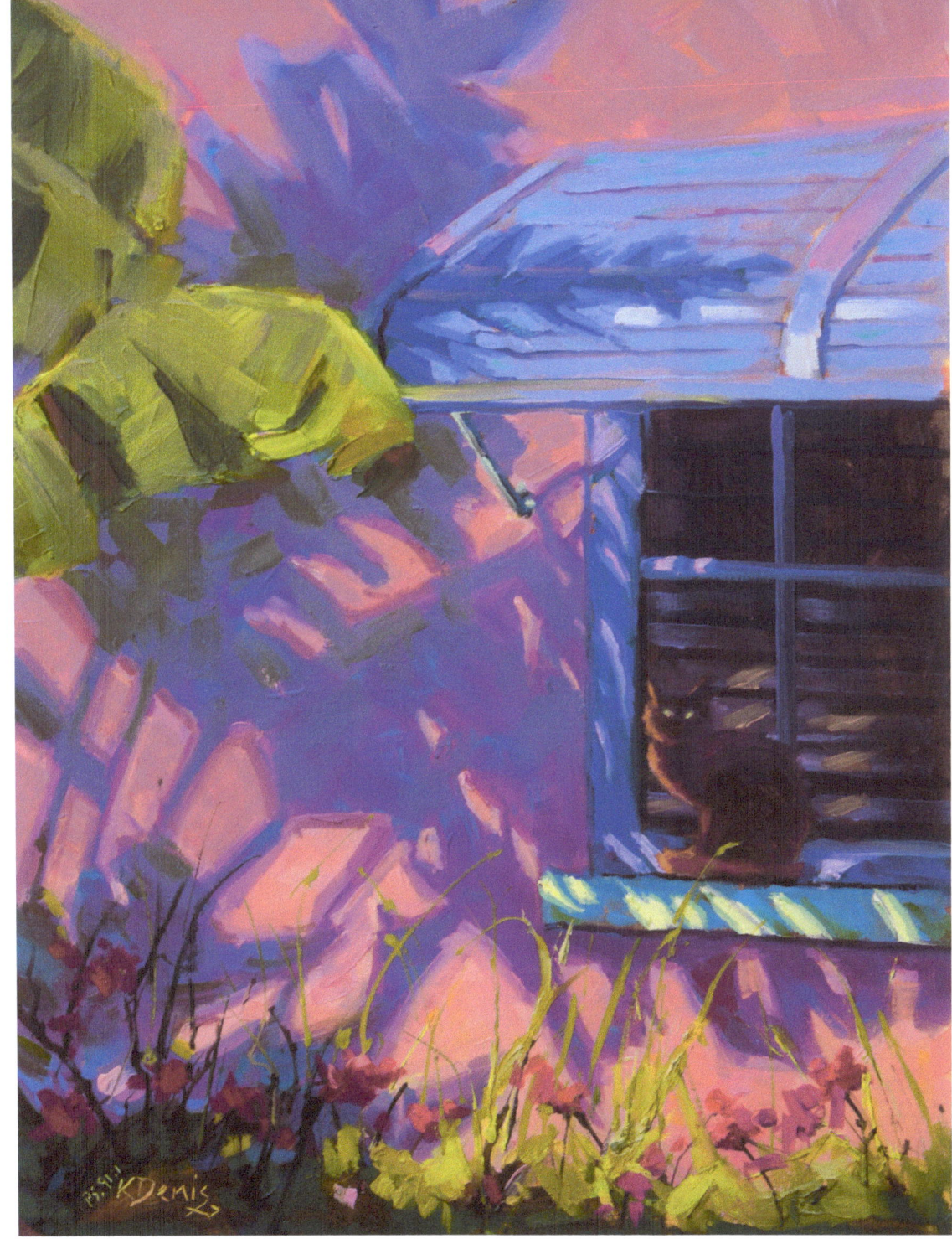

Kathleen Denis

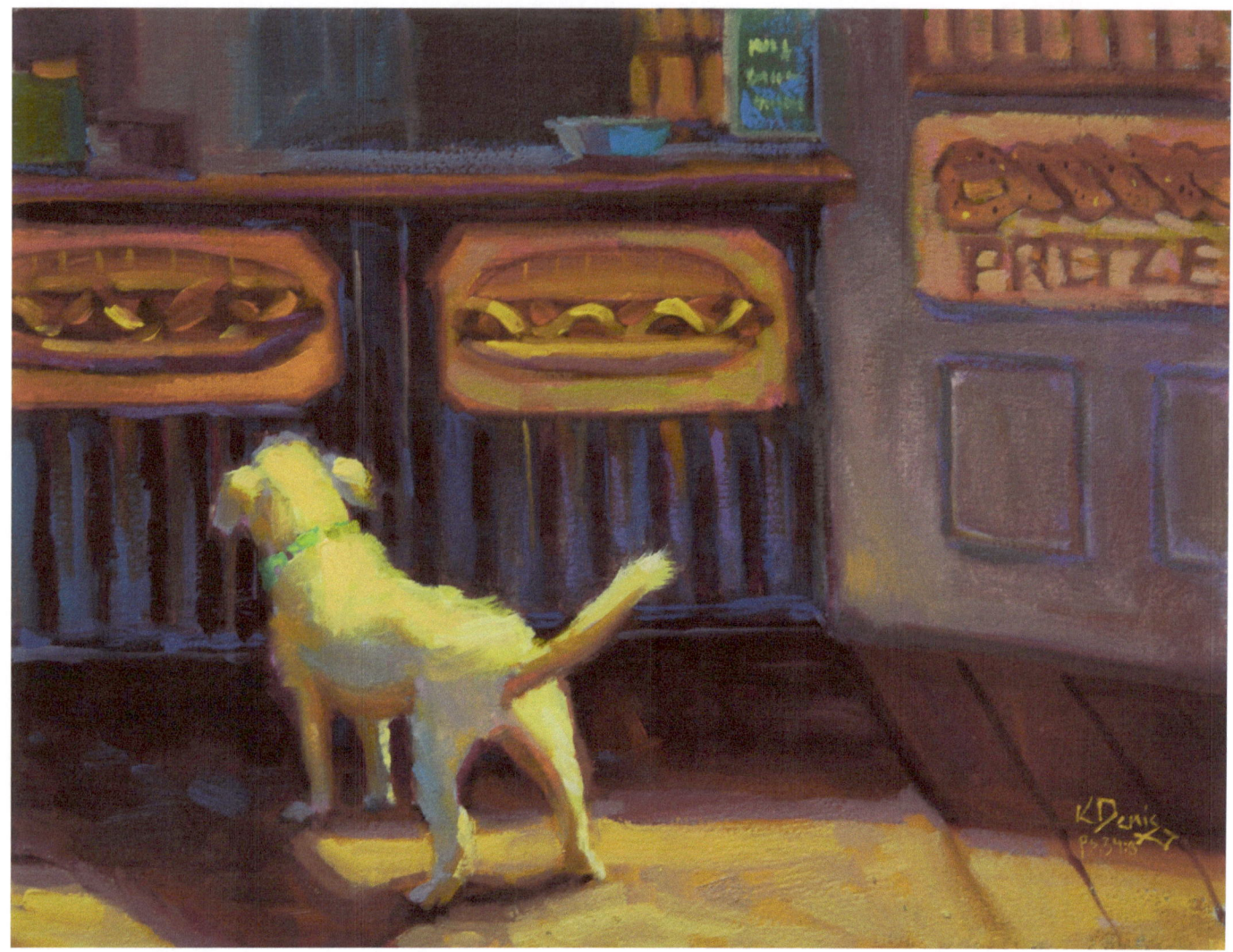

ANOTHER DOG PLEASE 9X12, OIL ON PANEL

LOCATION: KEY WEST

There are some things in life that are too cute for words, and this dog is one of them. On one of our day trips to Key West, I captured this priceless scene of a dog buying a dog!!! LOL!

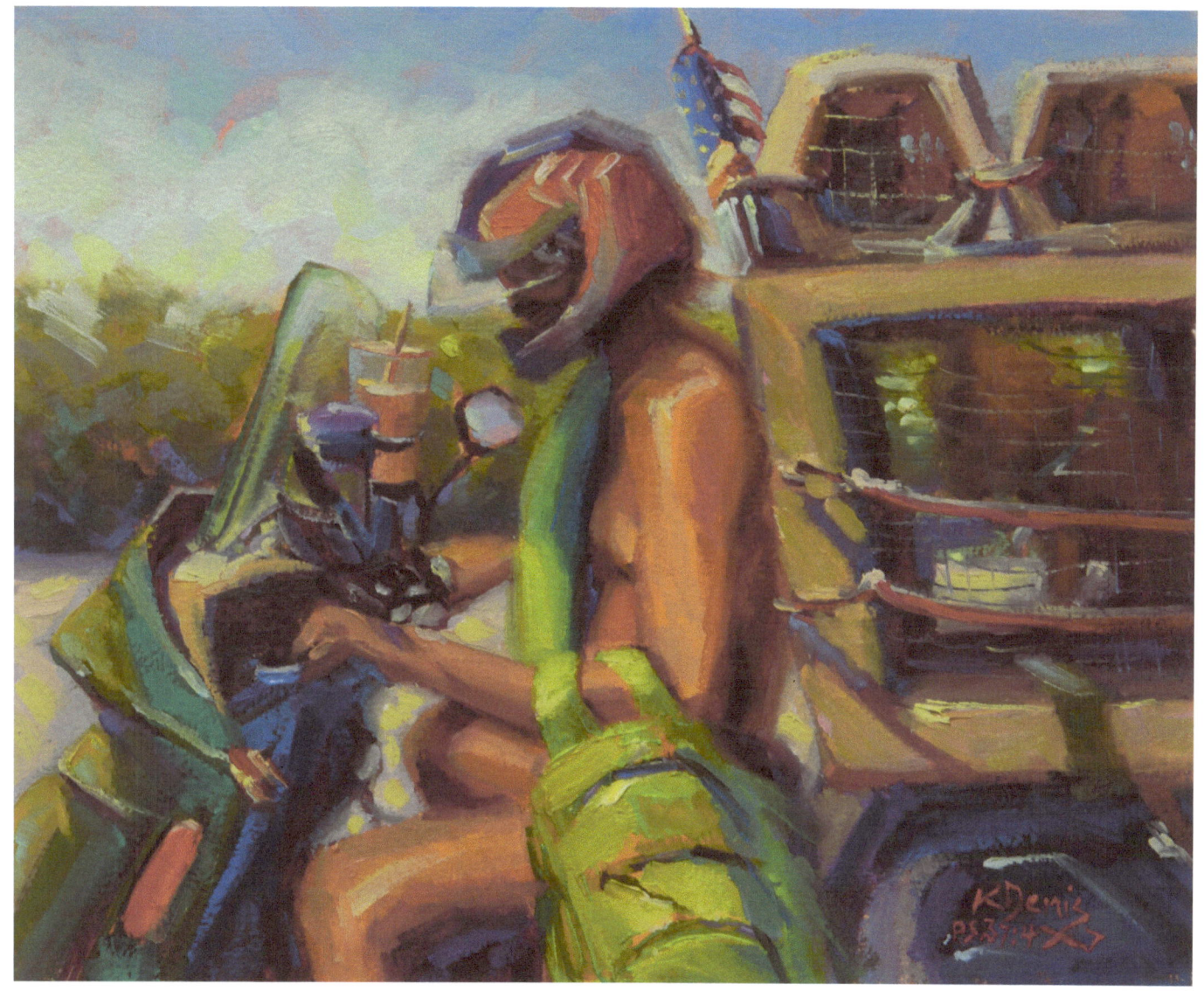

MAN ON A MISSION 8X10, OIL ON PANEL

LOCATION: OVERSEAS HIGHWAY

Unusual sightings in the Florida Keys are frequently seen. Yes, this man drives his motorcycle around with animals in cages. My husband Jeff and I often find ourselves saying: "Only in the Keys!"

Kathleen Denis

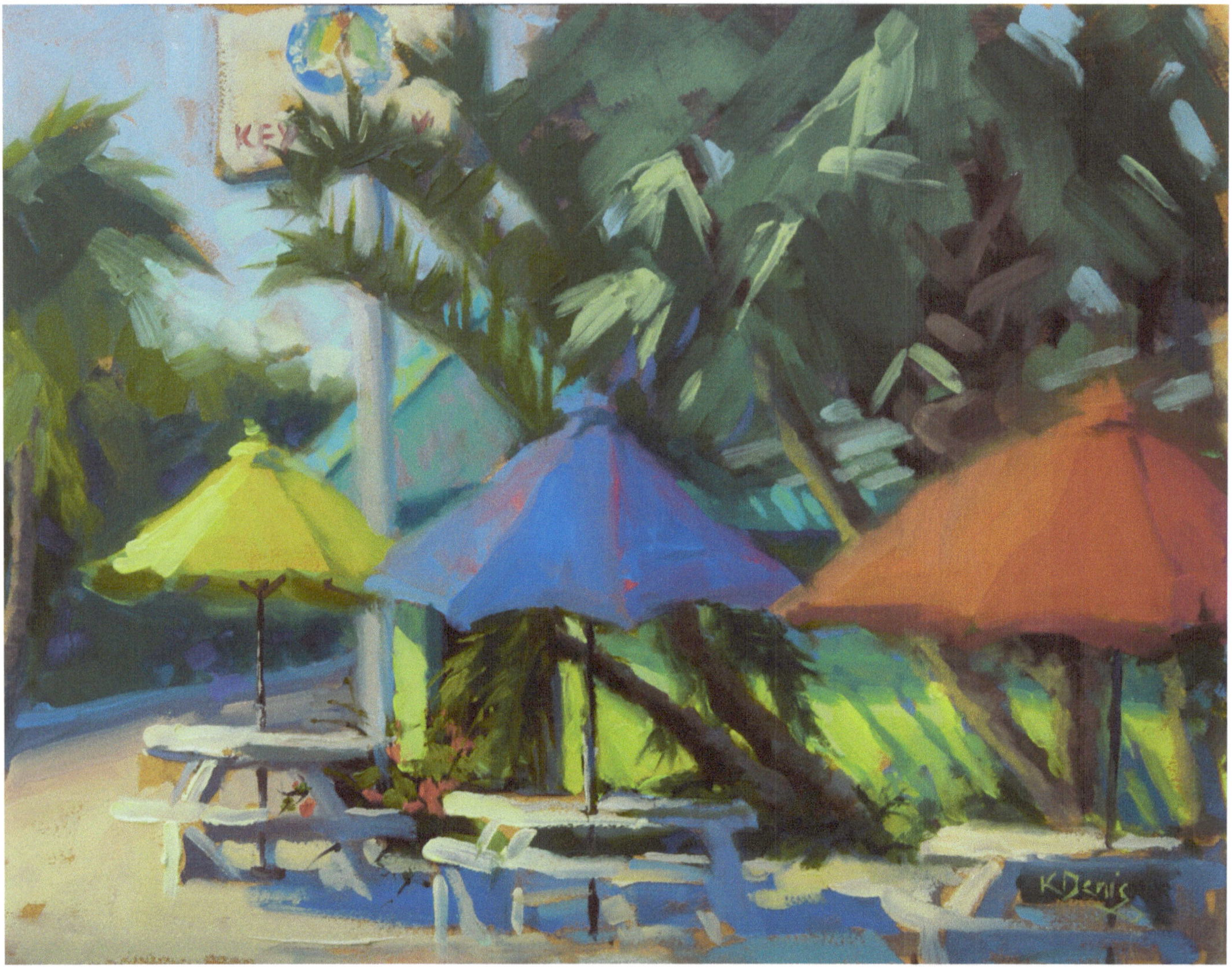

PROVISION 9X12, OIL ON PANEL

LOCATION: BLOND GIRAFFE, TAVERNIER

Every time I drive past the Blond Giraffe, the tropical colors of the building and umbrellas beckon me to paint them. Key lime, turquoise, blue and orange—a perfect Keys color combination!

Blond Giraffe produces some of the finest Key Lime products in the Keys. It is home of the famous Key Lime Pie, as well as fresh baked cookies, candies and the pie on a stick. Tania and Roberto, dear friends of ours, started with their first location in Key West and recently relocated to Tavernier. *Extreme Yummm!* [www.blondgiraffe.com.]

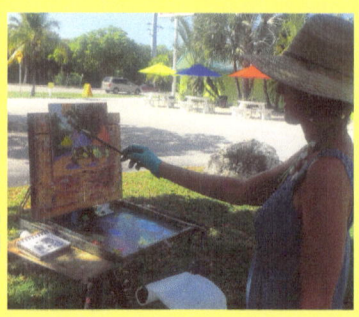

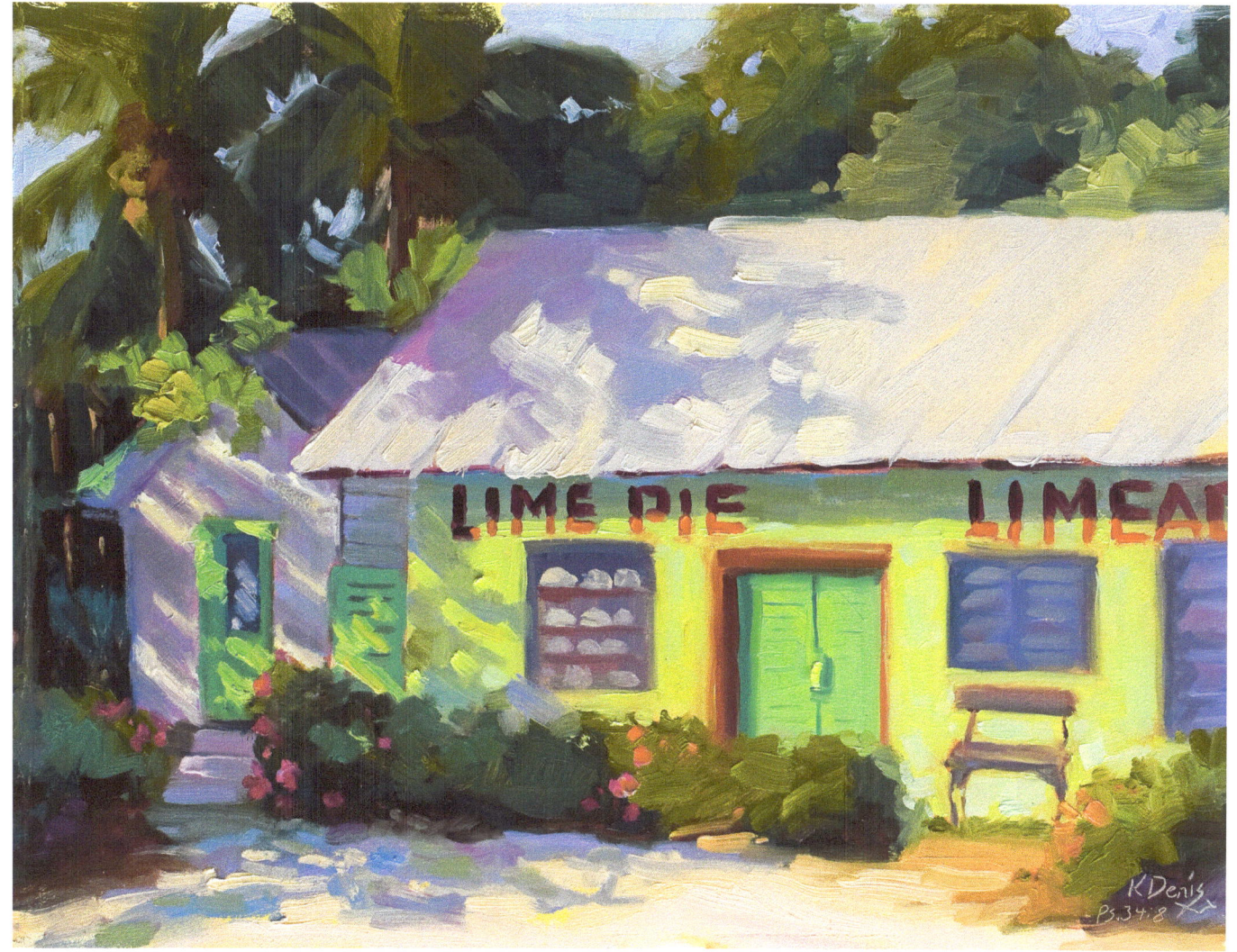

KEY LIME NOSTALGIA 12X16, OIL ON PANEL

LOCATION: 86560 OVERSEAS HIGHWAY, ISLAMORADA

The Key Lime Grill, as it was known in the 70s and 80s, is characteristic of old Florida Keys charm with a vibrant tropical palette. Built in 1928, it no longer operates as the place I often stopped as a teen for fabulous Key Lime pie, but now only has the façade and memories of days past.

*Historic information provided by Barbara Edgar. www.MatecumbeHistoricalTrust.com

Kathleen Denis

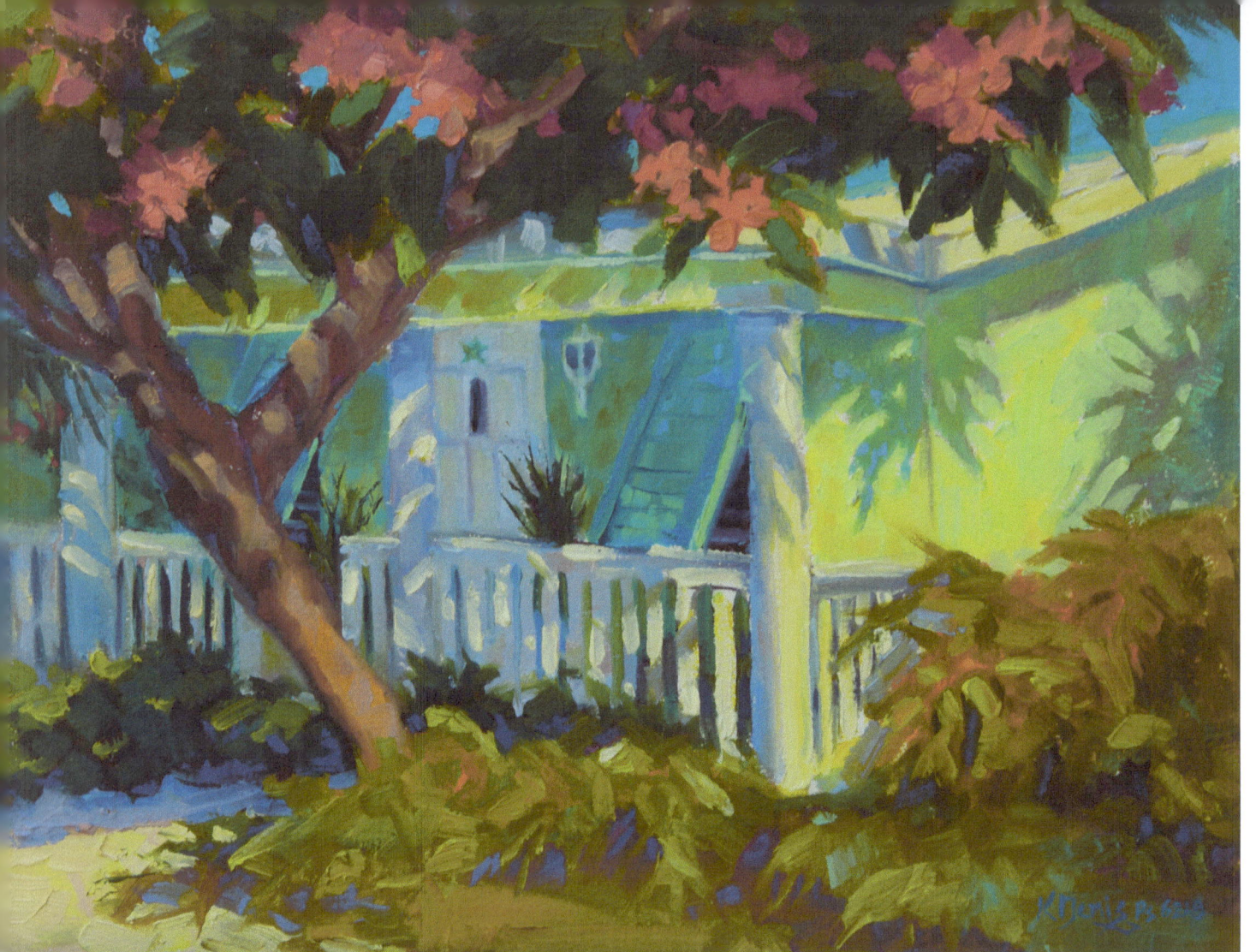

FRANGIPANI IN BLOOM 9X12, OIL ON PANEL

LOCATION: 88100 OVERSEAS HIGHWAY, ISLAMORADA

In the Keys, we really do have seasons other than hot and hurricane. Springtime brings about many breathtaking blossoms, one of which is the Frangipani Tree. As I was driving down the highway, the way the light was cast onto the brilliant colors caught my eye, and I knew I had to capture it on canvas.

[RIGHT] My "crazy" block in colors for Frangipani In Bloom are based on warm colors in the light, and cool colors in the shadows.

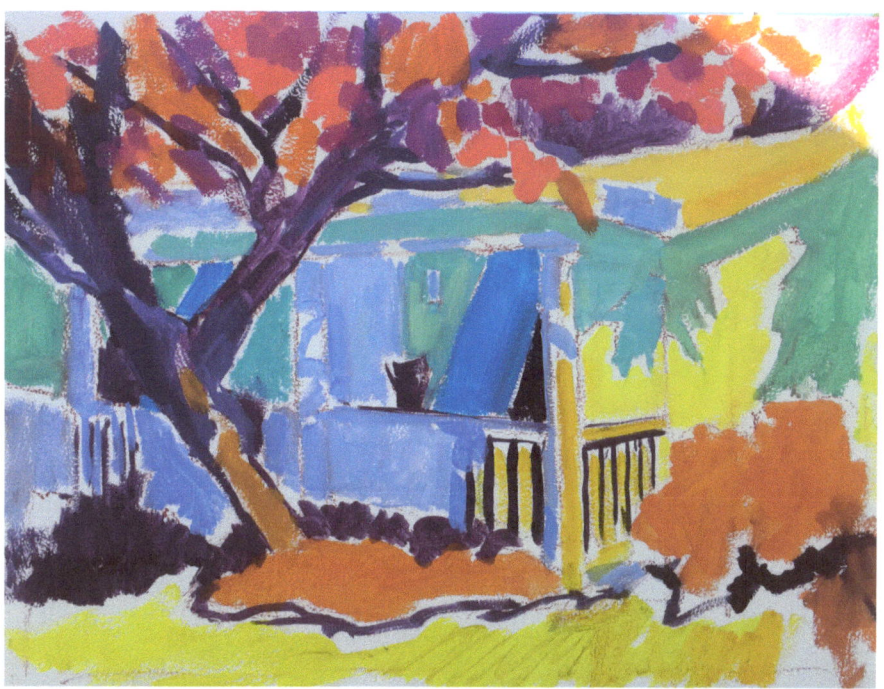

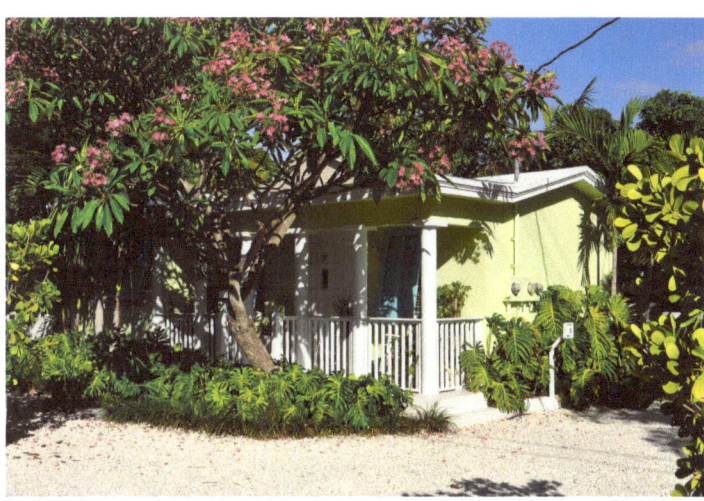

[TOP] Painting on location at this charming Keys Cottage helps me see the glowing colors much better than if I used a reference photo.

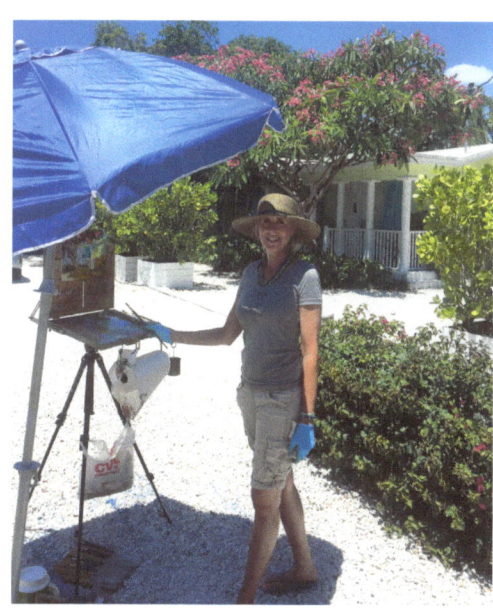

[TOP] Sunscreen and umbrella—a must on such a sunny day like this.

Kathleen Denis

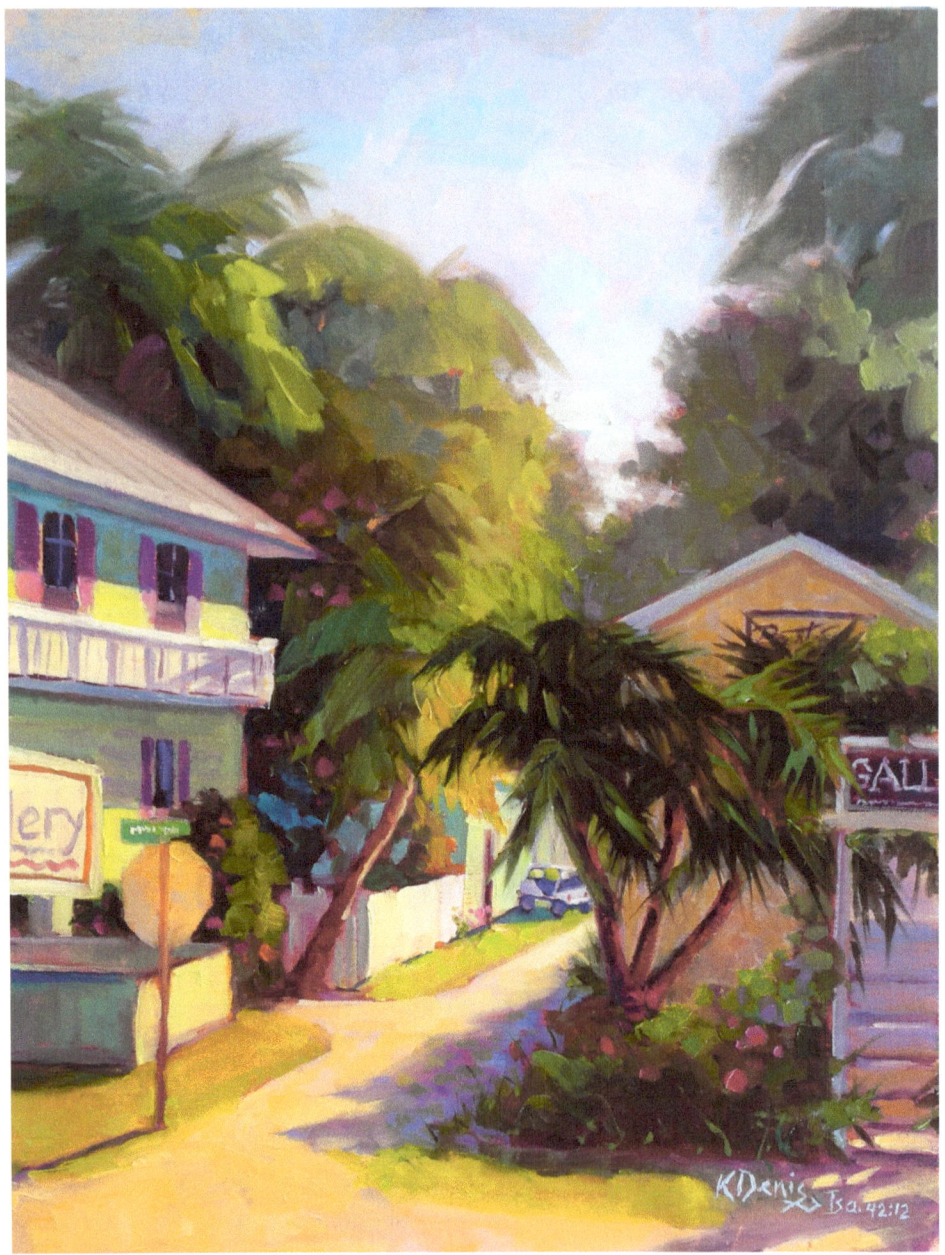

LOCATION: MORADA WAY ARTS & CULTURAL DISTRICT, 151 MORADA WAY, MILE MARKER 81

Art is good for the heart! As a result of Islamorada's fast growing art community, the well needed and amazing "Morada Way Art District" was birthed.

In addition to hosting the annual Paradise Paint Out, they feature monthly Third Thursday ArtWalks, art classes and special events throughout the year in various art mediums for all ages.

Redbone Gallery, with owners Gary and Susan Ellis, located at 200 Morada Way, host many fine artist's works, including mine for the past 20 years. Some paintings from this book may be found there.

Pasta Signature Gallery and Gallery Morada both sit on the entrance corners, with Morada Way Clay and others in between. It's a must see for all art lovers and collectors.

MORADA WAY
14X11, OIL ON PANEL

I was honored to paint this scene for Morada Way's use in brochures and advertisements.

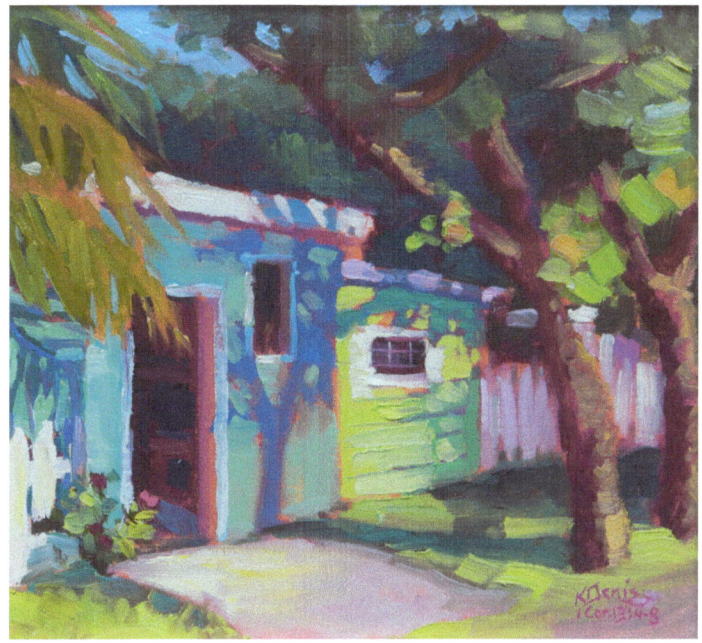

MAN CAVE
8X10, OIL ON PANEL

This present gallery space was once affectionately known as Dick Hagood's "Man Cave", the Director and founder of Morada Way Art District.

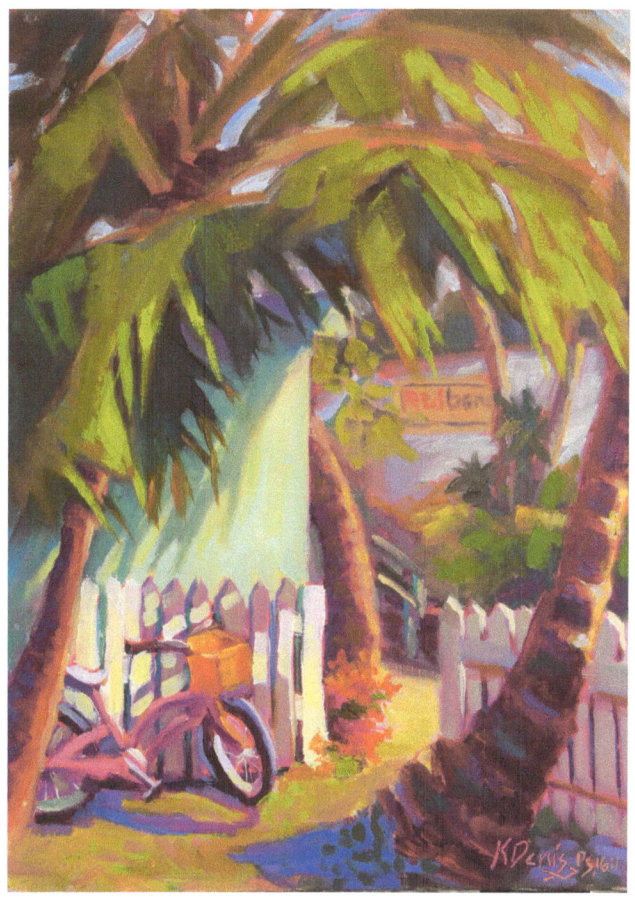

MORADA GARDEN VIEW
14X11, OIL ON LINEN PANEL

A garden in paradise is found tucked just behind the Gallery Morada, where organic veggies are grown and sold to local restaurants, culinary classes are given in the tropical style outdoor kitchen, and meetings are held amidst the lush gardens.

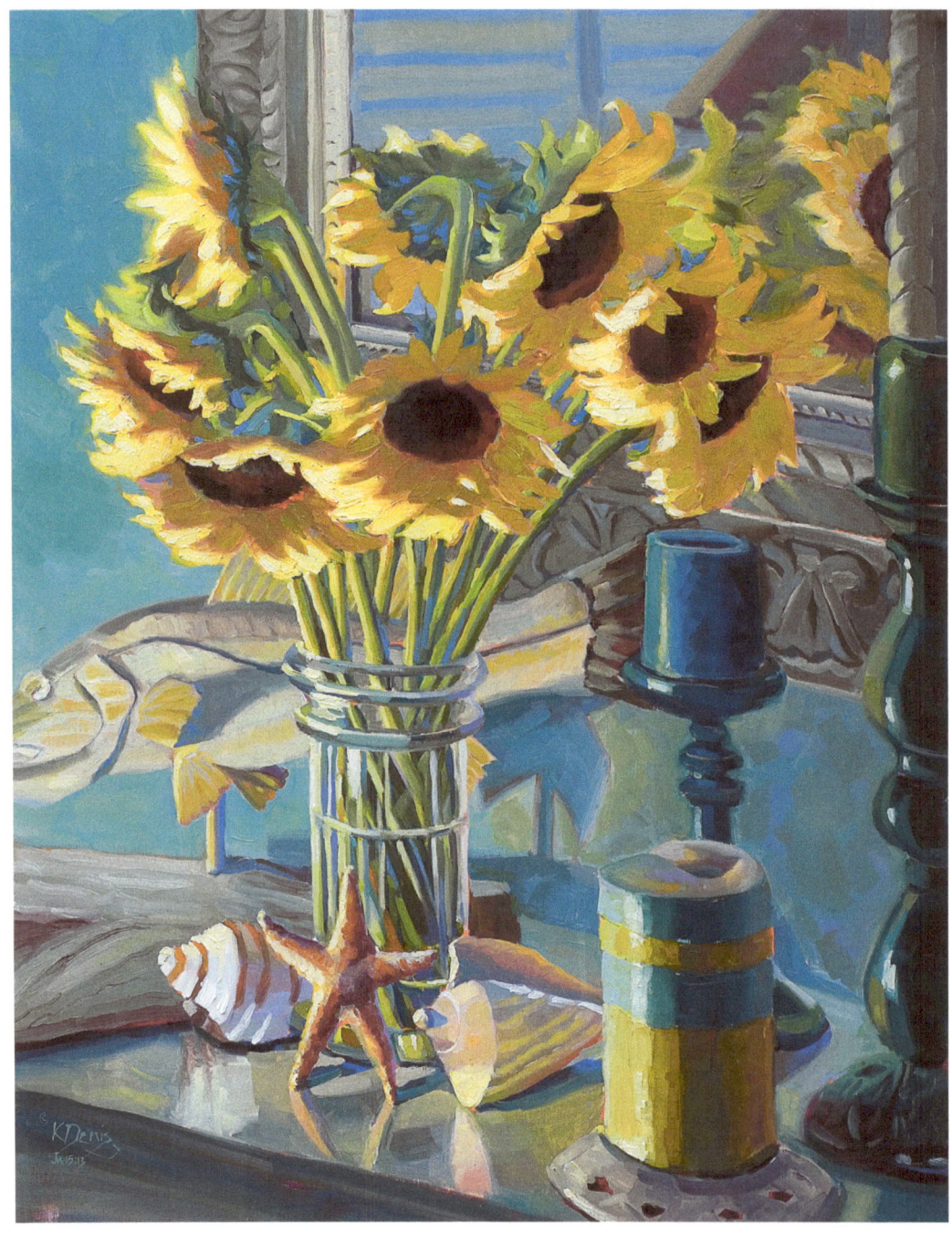

SUN AND SEA
30X24, OIL ON PANEL

LOCATION:
IN MY LIVING ROOM

Not painting these dazzling sunflowers received from a friend was not an option.

Though smells of paint and turpentine mingled with dinner a few nights, along with my easel adorning our living room floor, the afternoon sun shining through the window allowed for the perfect effect I longed to depict.

LESLIE'S PLACE
30X24,
OIL ON PANEL

LOCATION:
PLANTATION KEY
COLONY

As I came around the corner on a power walk, the most electrifying color of pink bougainvillea beckoned me to capture it on canvas.

Although the temperatures were well in the high 90s, I set up shop for the next three mornings, painting and enjoying meeting curious neighbors.

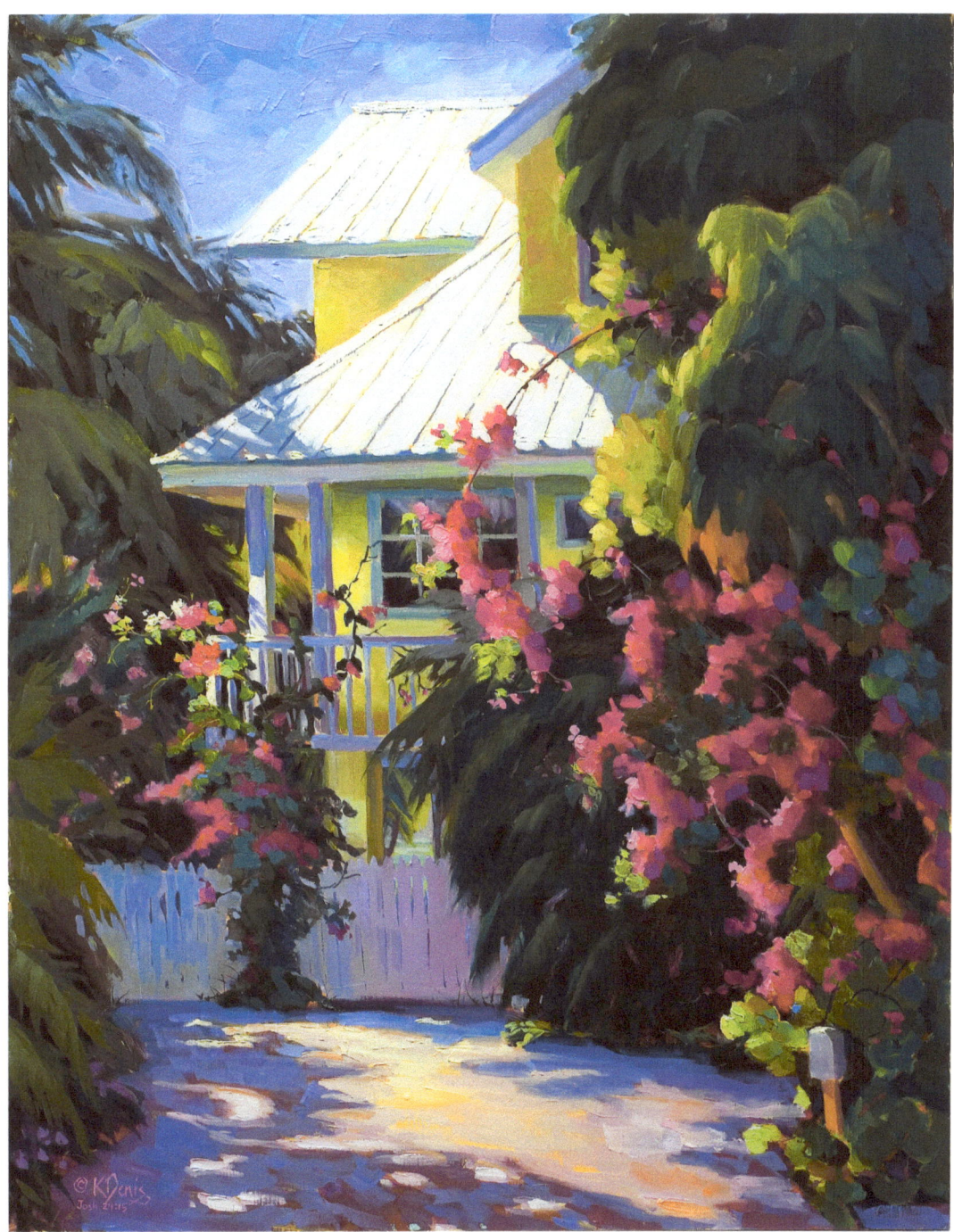

Kathleen Denis

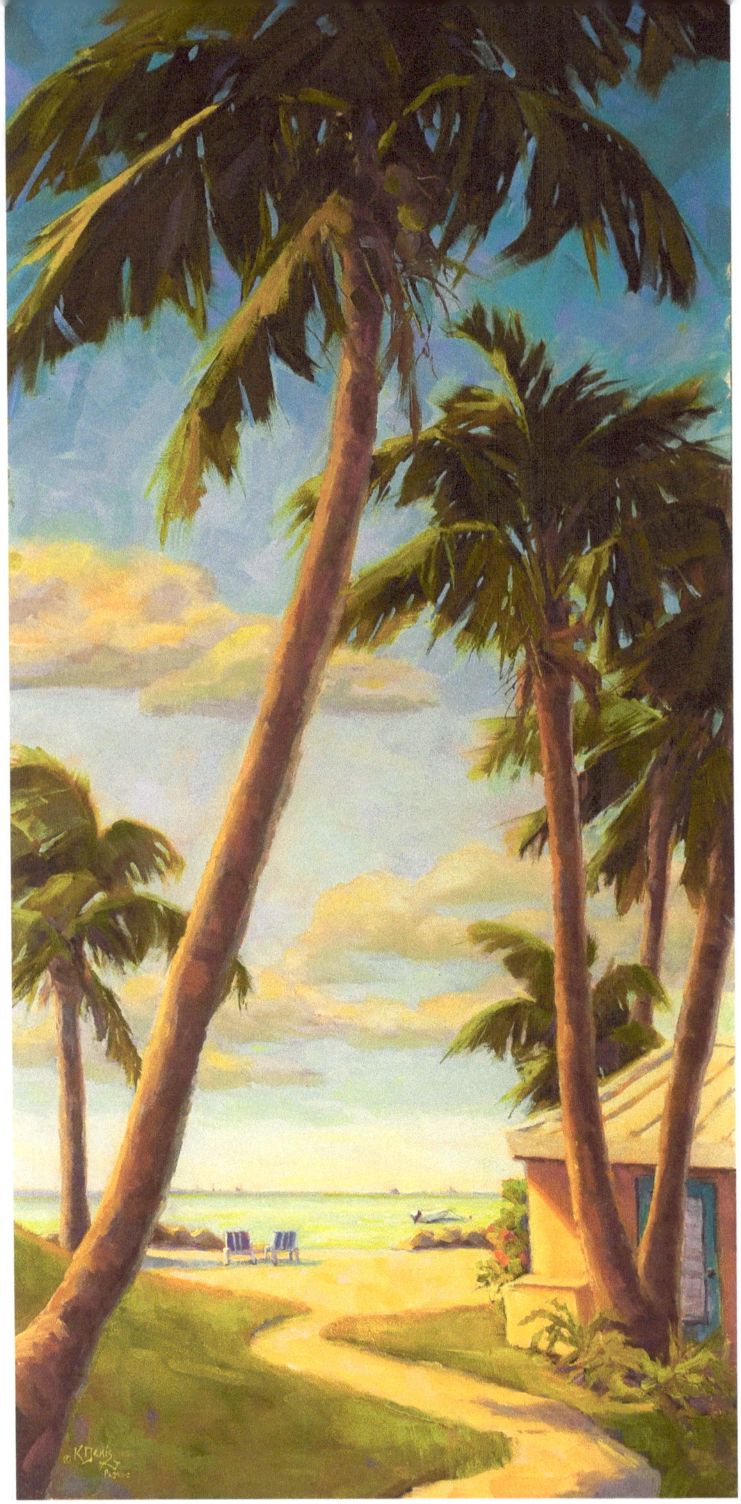

LOCATION: THE ISLANDER RESORT, ISLAMORADA—MILE MARKER 82

The Islander Resort, located on 22 acres, is one of my favorite painting locations as it offers a variety of interesting subjects, including 1300 feet of oceanfront, rental boats and kayaks, along with plenty of palm trees and hammocks. What more can you ask for?

ISLAND DAY 36X18, OIL ON PANEL

I love this inviting tropical view but I picked an extremely windy day to paint it. The canvas kept blowing off the easel, causing me to paint it sitting on the ground. You may be able to still find some twigs in it!

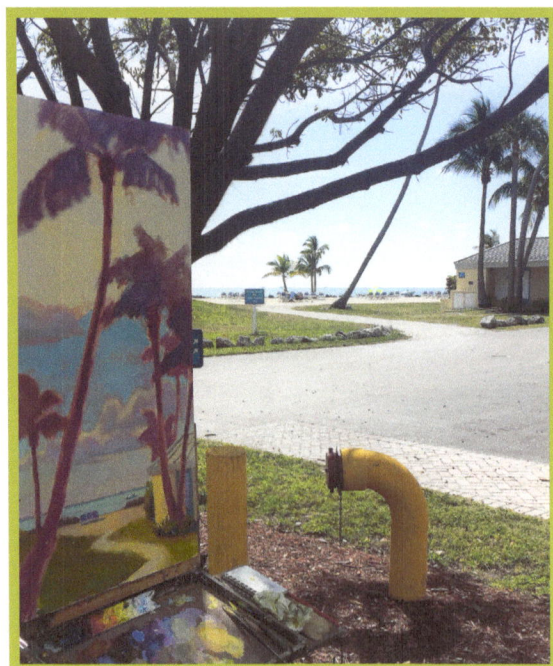

My office view today!

VACATION COTTAGE
24X18,
OIL ON PANEL

As the sun was setting in the west, I painted quickly to capture the intense light and shadows casted on these *vacation cottages* at the Islander Resort.

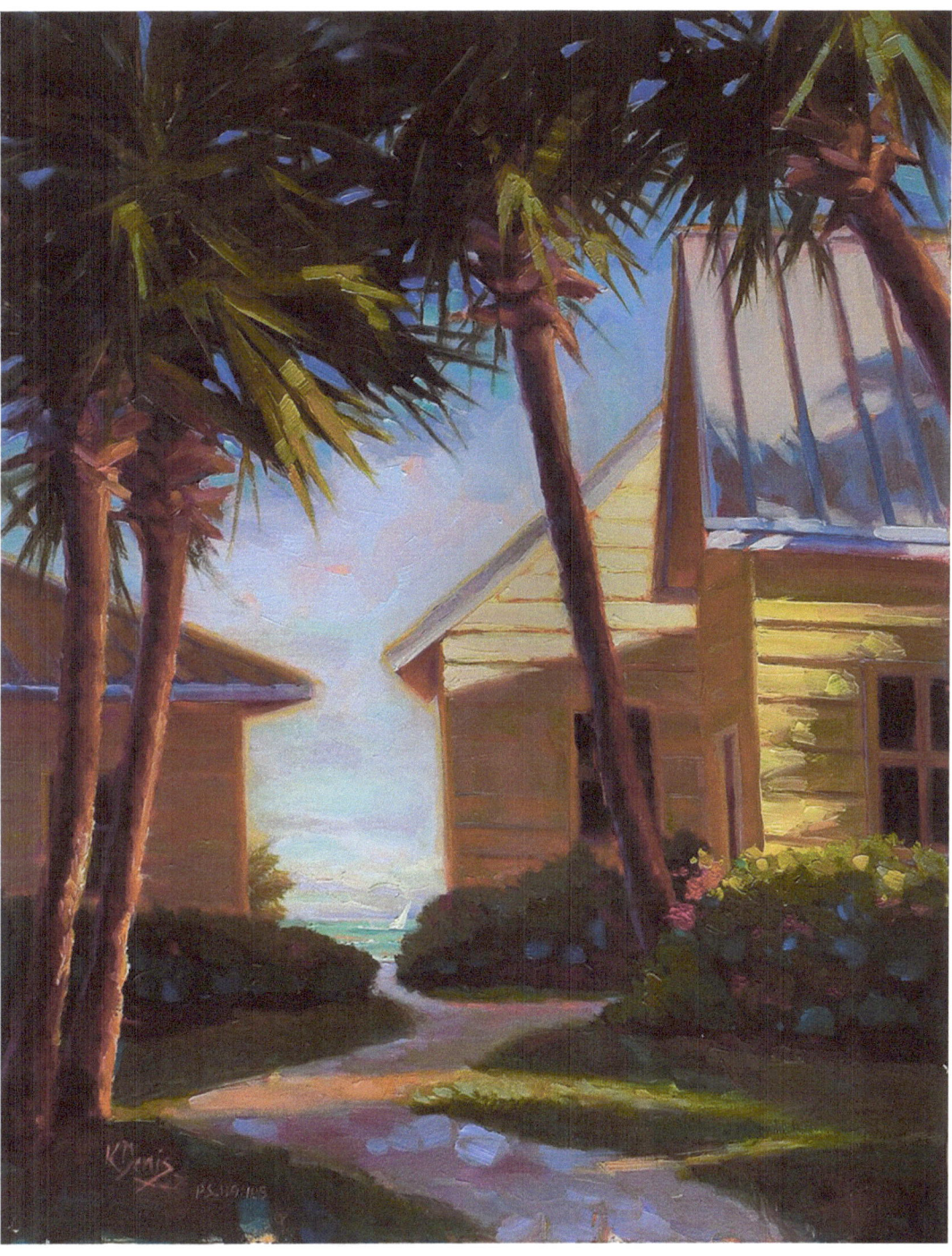

Kathleen Denis

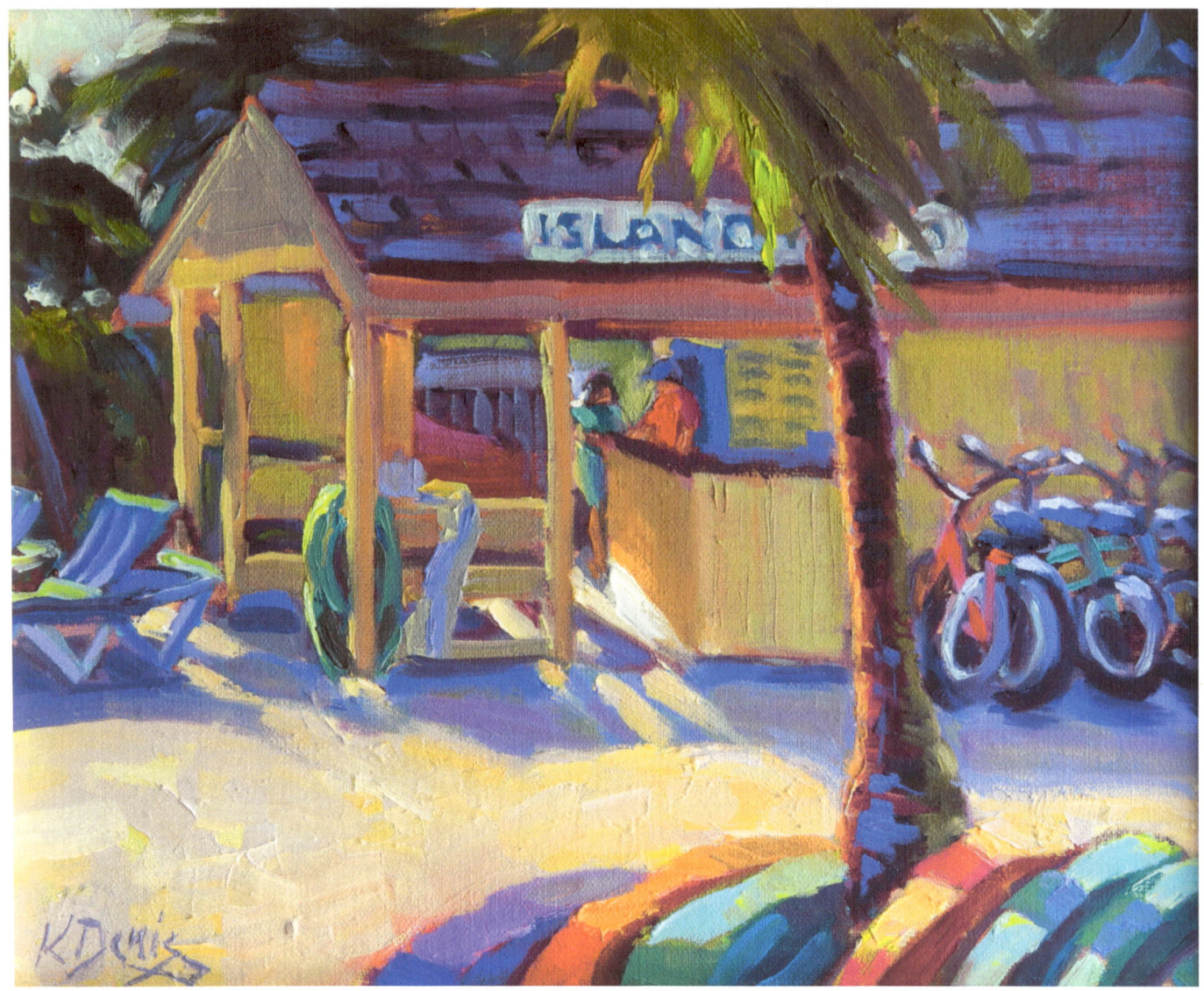

ISLANDER BEACH 8X10, OIL ON PANEL

By the beach, at the south end of the Islander Resort property, I discovered a great assortment of recreational rentals, which made for a fun and colorful painting.

PLEIN AIR AFFAIR
By Wally McCall

She stands before her easel where the linen board is fixed,
Upon her pallet, brilliant colors waiting to be mixed.
A metal pot of Turpenoid is dangling from a hook,
And a roll of paper towels is clutched within her elbow's crook.
Her paint brush fidgets anxiously and twitches in her hand,
To the beat heard through her earbuds by some island reggae band.
The sun breaks the horizon and illuminates her world,
With stripes of light and shadow like Old Glory's been unfurled.
Her brush darts to her oils like a heron spearing fish,
Then she waves it in a circle with a jaunty kind of swish.
She first begins the outline of the scene she will portray,
As she stands there sweating bullets the remainder of the day.
While she lays out her darkest darks and then her lightest lights,
The mosquito horde descends and starts inflicting itchy bites.
So she fires up her Thermacell and slathers on some Deet,
Which she applies with gusto from her forehead to her feet.
She continues underpainting using energetic strokes
And is unaware she has attracted quite a crowd of folks,

Until they start in asking her a multitude of questions,
Critique her work and offer her their uninformed suggestions.
She then applies the shapes and values of her composition,
The temperature of colors, adding depth to her rendition.
The illusion of perspective and the forms in third dimension,
Prompting her decision and demanding her attention.
The sun beats down high overhead. She dons a broad brimmed hat,
And adjusts her small umbrella but she never paused or sat.
She continues pushing paint around, a vast array of hues:
The cadmiums and pthalos, the yellows, reds, and blues.

Then finally, she finishes and thinks she got it right,
Portraying shapes and surfaces affected by the light.
The gallery is crowded as she peers across the hall,
And spies her painting hanging in the light upon the wall.
Behold! Upon the label is a bright red dot applied,
She has sold it. Someone loves it. And her heart swells up
with pride!

Wally McCall
Jupiter, FL
wbmccall@aol.com

Kathleen Denis

"When I paint,
I feel the presence
of God in my life."
—Kathleen Denis

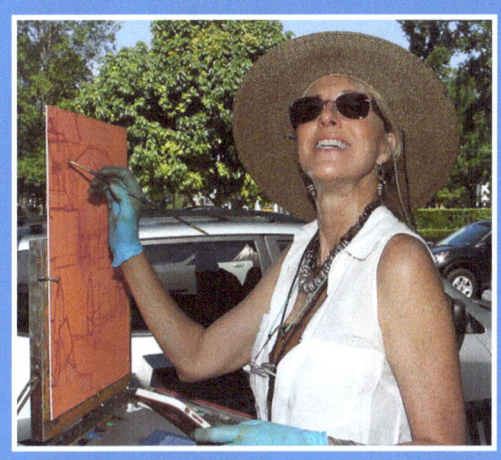

"I have filled him with the
Spirit of God...to make artistic
designs." —Exodus 31:3-4

www.ingramcontent.com/pod-product-compliance
Lightning Source LLC
Chambersburg PA
CBHW050803180526
45159CB00004B/1533